Another "first" from Woman's Press in the publishing of social work books. This is the first comprehensive history of neighborhood organization, brought to the fore by Sidney Dillick and analyzed in the light of its history and its future.

One of the most characteristic and important hallmarks of democracy has been the voluntary association of citizens into self-governed groups, in order to enhance the common good and to solve specific social problems at the *local* level. It has been felt that strong local neighborhood groups and councils help decentralize authority and bring it closer to the people.

Dr. Dillick traces the history of commu- neighborhood and izations for defense services, those which have been formed to strengthen our educational system and those designed to develop other aspects of community welfare. A comprehensive bibliography has been included for those who wish to explore further into this fascinating field of social work.

This book has been planned to provide inspiration and *concrete* help to all those volunteers who invest so much of their time and money to serve as members of boards and committees for community organizations. It should be essential reading for staffs of social agencies, and for students of sociology and social work.

COMMUNITY ORGANIZATION FOR NEIGHBORHOOD DEVELOPMENT— PAST AND PRESENT

Community Organization
for
Neighborhood Development—
Past and Present

By SIDNEY DILLICK, Ph.D., M.S.W.

WOMAN'S PRESS

WHITESIDE, INC.

AND

WILLIAM MORROW & COMPANY

New York · 1953

HV
41
.D5

To my father and mother

ALEXANDER DILLICK

ANNE PIKE DILLICK

ACKNOWLEDGMENTS

THIS book is itself an acknowledgment of contributions to community organization for neighborhood development. Students of community organization are heavily indebted to those persons whose activities, ideas, and feelings have contributed to the understanding of neighborhood life and to the development of agencies, programs, and methods for dealing with the problems of family living in metropolitan areas. The ability of pioneers in neighborhood organization to relate the needs and interests of people to the social problems and values of their times is a striking feature of the record.

The present work was originally conceived some years ago when I was on the staff of the Welfare Council of Toronto, which also served the surrounding district. The devoted leadership which Miss Bessie Touzel gave to the Council as its Executive Secretary inspired me to pursue, at a later date, systematic study of community organization as a field and as a social work method. As staff consultant to local community councils I became associated with Miss Violet M. Sieder, of Community Chests and Councils, Inc., whose vision and tireless energy were opening many eyes to the significance of community councils for health and welfare planning in metropolitan areas. Subsequent acquaintance with many people active in the widespread community council movement has contributed to my interest in exploring this subject.

While I was attending the University of Pittsburgh School

of Social Work my impression of the significance of the community council movement grew considerably. Although every part of the School's program has had its effect on the writing of this book, I wish to acknowledge particularly my debt to Dean Wilber I. Newstetter and to Professors Marion Hathway, Ruth E. Smalley, and Gertrude Wilson, at that time members of the faculty. Dean Newstetter's interest and help, as Dean and as teacher of new ideas on social work practice in community organization, have been major factors in carrying out this project.

Through the interest of Dean Newstetter, Miss Sieder, and Mr. Ralph H. Blanchard, Executive Director of Community Chests and Councils, Inc., the need for an historical study of neighborhood community organization was brought to the attention of Russell Sage Foundation. As a result the Foundation's Department of Social Work Administration asked me to prepare a report on this subject. Dr. Donald S. Howard, then Director of the Department, was responsible for arrangements which were highly conducive to carrying out the study. This is the completed report, which was also submitted to the University of Pittsburgh School of Social Work in partial fulfillment of the requirements for the degree of Master of Social Work.

Grateful acknowledgment is made for the many kinds of help I have received from Russell Sage Foundation. During the early stages the Foundation made it possible for me to spend full time on the project for three months, provided office facilities, clerical and research assistance, and unusual library service. The help of several staff members, in searching for relevant data through vast quantities of published material, and in preparing notes and manuscript, is recalled with warm appreciation. Dr. Howard's interest, encouragement, and incisive editorial criticism have been invaluable. I appreciate especially his willingness to continue his help for some time after he left his post at the Foundation until the project was substantially completed. The consideration shown by Dr. Donald Young, General Director, through a period of major change in the Foundation's program, and the help of the Foundation in making publication possible under these circumstances, are much appreciated.

Permission to reprint material in this book is acknowledged from the following organizations and publishers: Survey Associates, New York: for *The Commons,* May, 1901; for *The Pittsburgh Survey* (Volume on the Pittsburgh District, Civic Frontage), 1914; for the *Journal of Social Forces,* December, 1925. Community Service Society of New York: for New York City Charity Organization Society, "Twenty-fifth Annual Report," 1907. National University Extension Association: for *Proceedings of the National University Extension Association,* Chicago, 1919. University of Pennsylvania Press, Philadelphia: for Marion Elderton, ed., *Case Studies of Unemployment,* 1931. Acknowledgment is also made to the many others whose material is cited and whose names appear in the footnotes accompanying the text.

A careful reading of the manuscript, generously undertaken by Mrs. Nina M. Coveney, resulted in numerous suggestions which improved the readability of the text. For typing of the manuscript in its final stages appreciation is expressed to Mrs. Mildred Levin and Mrs. Anita Vargas Amagna. Miss Shirley G. Hale very kindly helped with the reading of proof.

While acknowledging the many contributions of others I accept sole responsibility for what appears in these pages, particularly for shortcomings.

The encouragement and sustaining patience of my wife, Filomena Florendo Dillick, has made this work a labor of love from beginning to end.

SIDNEY DILLICK

Cranston, Rhode Island
April 7, 1953

TABLE OF CONTENTS

INTRODUCTION

VARIOUS CLAIMS have been made for the neighborhood approach to some of the problems of living in large cities. Some persons have said that strong local neighborhood associations or councils will help to decentralize authority and bring it closer to the people. Specialists in adult education see merit in neighborhood organization for citizenship education. Settlement leaders feel it will help develop the friendliness and neighborliness that is lacking in urban communities. City planners see in neighborhood organization an effective means by which local community consciousness can be aroused to put life into plans for clusters of neighborhoods in large cities. Social workers think of it as enabling a community to tackle some of its own problems directly.

In carrying out the neighborhood approach many different forms of organization are possible. Some of these can be applied to an individual neighborhood while others are applicable to the larger area of the district which includes several neighborhoods. A committee of social agency representatives may set up an area project for coordinating their services to prevent delinquency. A council of delegates from the various organizations in the neighborhood or district may be formed to promote a community recreation program. Groups of neighbors, or representatives of organizations, may join

15

forces to solve some specific neighborhood problem and disband when they have achieved their purpose.

A number of questions are being asked today about the function, structure, and operation of plans to "organize" the neighborhood. Who should provide the auspices? Should the resulting organizations seek to operate services themselves, or to coordinate at the neighborhood or district level the services of the Y's, the settlements, family and child welfare agencies, and the public welfare, recreation, and health departments?

Should an agency which offers direct service to individuals seek to coordinate its services with those of other such agencies? What part should be played in neighborhood organization by settlements, adult education organizations, and community welfare councils? Should neighborhood or district councils be developed? Should they consist of representatives of social agencies only, or of other organizations as well? Should they consist of individual members or delegates of organizations, or both? How should neighborhood or district councils be financed? What kind of staff service do they need, and what should the staff worker do? If these councils are to be developed as social planning bodies, how should they be related to the over-all community welfare council?

Much light can be shed upon these questions by an examination of past efforts at neighborhood organization viewed within the setting of their times. We can learn a great deal from the experience of the settlements, the charity organization societies, the school center movement, the public health projects, the defense councils of both world wars, the juvenile delinquency projects, and area and community councils.

For the proper perspective it is essential to review each of these movements from the inside, and in the light of the period in which it was active. It will also be helpful to see each historical period as a whole, so that the interrelation of the various movements will be apparent.

This study is designed to review the major developments in neighborhood organization for social welfare from the end of the Civil War to the era following World War II. The report begins with the industrial revolution because it brought about the economic and social changes that set the basic form of our social welfare problems. The opening section of each chapter reviews briefly the economic and social changes that have taken place since the industrial revolution. The social conditions that accompanied these changes seriously affected the functioning of society and the lives of individual persons. Since the neighborhood approach was used in various efforts to meet the material, social, and emotional needs evolving within the framework of the new society, this report focuses upon the development of certain phases of modern social work.

Neighborhood organization is not considered as a movement by itself; rather, it is thought of as a level of social welfare organization which takes on a particular form in a specific setting. Social welfare institutions have used various forms of neighborhood organization from the industrial revolution to the present day. These institutions sought to approach social welfare problems at the neighborhood level because that is where their incidence is seen most clearly. Some of these institutions were organized to deal with social problems over a large geographic area and sought to focus their efforts upon specific neighborhoods by means of neighborhood organization. Other institutions were organized on a neighborhood basis and sought to develop their work from within individual neighborhoods. From both types of effort there developed many of our health, welfare, education, and recreation services. Out of the need to coordinate these services councils of social agencies and, later, community welfare councils developed. The neighborhood or district community council evolved as a means of achieving this coordination at the neighborhood and district levels.

Many examples of neighborhood organization will be presented. Significant projects have been included, as well as illustrations of widespread movements.

As we proceed from one period to another it will be important for us to note changes in the concept of the relationship between the individual and society. From the early concern of the "privileged" members of society to bring the "underprivileged" up to a certain standard of living and behavior, we have advanced to the concept that the means be provided whereby people can attain a socially desired standard of living and of life. Formerly, the individual in need of help from society was regarded as suffering from certain moral lacks and as being, therefore, beyond the pale of respectability. Today, as a result of democratic influences in and upon social work, we see him not as a moral outcast but as a person on whom certain socially undesirable conditions have impinged through no fault of his own. It is now generally recognized that every individual has a right to society's help and a right to participate in determining social policy. As a matter of fact, society has taken upon itself the obligation to help individuals to develop the capacity and the skills for participation in groups, as members and as leaders. Educators and social workers are very much concerned with this process in both formal and informal groups. The concept of the participating, responsible citizen who is at one and the same time the supporter and the recipient of community services, emerges simultaneously with the concept of social work as a professional service available for the sound development of the individuals, groups, and communities of which our society is composed.

The development of the professional practice of social work, particularly in the newer methods, is significant for our present purpose. Social work method recognizes that the individual has the right and the responsibility to determine his own course of action and to accept its consequences. To satisfy his own needs and interests he participates through voluntarily formed groups in activities directed to social goals. Intergroup organizations develop in which the representatives of groups work together on matters of concern to their groups. Two distinct processes are involved, which provide the bases for two methods of social work—social group work and social intergroup work. The former is concerned with the needs and interests of individuals and with the group goals toward which they are working together. The latter is concerned with helping the representatives of groups work together to formulate and achieve intergroup or community goals.[1] Due attention must be given to these two levels of integration of human effort, since neither alone can offer the key to neighborhood organization.

As we examine neighborhood organization activities it will be well to bear in mind their appropriate scope. In many instances the problems of the local community are caused by factors that are metropolitan, state, national, and international in their origin and often they are as widespread in their effect. Of what practical value is neighborhood action on problems of unemployment, dependency, housing, unless it is related to actions of sufficient size and scope? Tackling problems at the neighborhood level which cannot be solved or significantly affected by neighborhood action leads to disappointment and frustration. On the other hand, neighborhood organization will not be very significant if the objectives attained are of minor importance. Nor will it have much significance if we overestimate the value of efforts to change social norms in neighborhoods where social conditions such as low incomes, unemployment, and substandard housing bring economic dependency and ill-health.

[1] Newstetter, Wilber I., "The Social Intergroup Work Process: How Does It Differ from the Social Group Work Process?" in Howard, Donald S., ed., *Community Organization, Its Nature and Setting,* New York: American Association of Social Workers, Association for the Study of Community Organization, Community Chests and Councils, Inc., 1947.

Special attention is given to coordinating and planning because the services which society makes available are offered by numerous agencies under various auspices. In our large cities community welfare councils are at work relating needs to services in the fields of health, welfare, and recreation, and are constantly working out the relative responsibilities of the public and the voluntarily supported agencies. Community chests are raising money for most of our voluntary agencies in a single annual campaign. More extensive and more effective participation of citizen organizations is being sought in these efforts.

This study was prompted by the need for more effective coordinated use of the social services and for greater citizen participation in community planning for social welfare. It was thought that by scanning the history of neighborhood organization laymen and professional workers might see current situations in perspective and find some illumination of today's problems in the experience of the past. The underlying hypotheses are that neighborhood organization has made and can continue to make a significant contribution to social welfare; that the neighborhood approach represents an important method by which direct-service agencies and community welfare councils can enlarge the constituency of social work, in terms both of those served and those participating in policy-making; that the concept of the neighborhood or district community council is one of the most comprehensive approaches to neighborhood organization today, especially when it is related to the city-wide community welfare council through which it helps to achieve coordinated planning and use of services by the whole community.

In this report we are concerned with the "neighborhood," "community," "district," and "area" as parts of cities and their metropolitan areas. There are significant sociological differences between urban and rural neighborhoods. No attempt is made to deal with the rural neighborhoods. Further, it is not intended to trace the history of neighborhood organization in specific cities. Examples are cited merely to present concrete instances of neighborhood organization in the context in which they occur.

In its specific sense "neighborhood" is used to denote a relatively small area such as that served by an elementary school; "district" denotes a larger area, containing several neighborhoods, such as that served by a high school. "Neighborhood" in its generic sense, as in the terms "neighborhood approach," "neighborhood organization," and "neighborhood council," refers to social welfare activities at the point where families live and have their being. This distinction between "neighborhood" and "district" has not had general acceptance throughout the periods under review, and as a result "neighborhood" is often used in the generic sense to denote both "neighborhood" and "district."

The term "neighborhood organization," as used here, refers to a level of organization and does not denote a method. The term "community organization" is used to denote method, whether at the neighborhood, district, city, county, state, national, or international level. We are concerned here with community organization for social welfare at the "neighborhood" and "district" levels.

CHAPTER I

"SETTLING" AND "VISITING"

A. Background: From the Industrial Revolution to 1900

1. *First Impact of the Industrial Revolution in England*

In order to understand today's questions in neighborhood organization for social welfare we must look at the historical background of our social welfare problems. Our starting point is the industrial revolution and the social conditions that accompanied it, first in England and later in this country.

With the rapid growth of cities and all the attendant effects of the industrial revolution in England, the village came to be extolled as the social unit of most manageable proportions for maintaining accepted social norms. The belief was current that by encouraging in the crowded cities the close personal relations between neighbors which were characteristic of the small town, much could be done to counteract the material and moral ravages of the industrial revolution.

Before the growth of the new industrial cities community life was such that everyone knew his neighbors well. Later, however, families could live next door to one another without manifesting any neighborly spirit. It was difficult for community life to develop, since neighbors came from widely separated points, standards of conduct varied, and frequent moving made constant readjustments necessary. Instead of an entire family working within the home as it once did, its various members now had jobs outside, each one associated with different people, and enjoyed different activities. Small children frequently missed the care and affection of mothers away at work all day. Often there were boarders to complicate family relations.

The personal relations of domestic industry, the guilds, and the feudal manor were replaced by the impersonal relations of the factory. Men, women, and very often little children spent long hours in unsanitary surroundings. Home, overcrowded, often became merely a place to eat and sleep in a monotonous round of existence. And through all this ran the fear of losing one's job.

Who were these people who crowded around the factories for a money wage and the greater freedom it brought? They came from the English countryside. Some were apprentices and journeymen left without a means of livelihood after the breakup of the guilds. Many of them were "paupers," children and adults who came from the almshouses. With the increasing division of labor, skill was no prerequisite.

The new factory system increased the productivity of human labor. For the first time many commodities became available to millions of people. Industrial progress brought about "the separation of the shop from the house and the restoration of the home to the family." [1] There was a great advance in the availability of public education. A new emphasis was given to social and political life by the increasing importance of the voluntary association, which provided opportunities for close personal relations.

[1] Taylor, Graham, "Social Tendencies of the Industrial Revolution," *The Commons*, October, 1904, p. 461.

2. Industrial Revolution in the United States

In this country the industrial revolution gained impetus in the decades following the Civil War. At the turn of the century, when great advances were being made in science and communication, "the rapid sweep of corporate business . . . crashed the gates of our old individualism and left a great wake of rankled feelings along with its scrap of life and limb." [2] This prodded men into a re-examination of established social institutions. It gave a critical edge to investigations and an insurgent temper to social movements.

Meanwhile the tremendous influx of immigration created many problems in American communities. Municipal governments were weak; the division of powers between the state and federal governments left the responsibility for initiative to the states, communities, and citizens.

Victims of the new factory system banded together to demand higher wages and better working conditions. Trade unions developed. Laws were passed for the protection of the "disadvantaged classes."

While on the one hand there was great deprivation, great fortunes were being amassed and much new wealth was being created by the new productive system. The contrast pricked many consciences. The new system, it was thought, could not be disturbed, but something could be done to ameliorate its adverse effects.

Stuart Queen in his *Social Work in the Light of History*[3] has pointed out that "business" and "philanthropy" were kept separate. Control of the industrial system could not be yielded to those who suffered under it and who wished to change it, but "gifts" to the unfortunates could be made. Much of the sentimentalism characteristic of the philan-

[2] Kellogg, Paul U., "Our Hidden Cities and the American Zest for Discovery," *Survey Graphic*, LX, July 1, 1928, p. 391.
[3] Philadelphia: J. B. Lippincott, 1922, p. 87.

thropic work of this period was fostered by financing ameliorative measures for the victims of the system out of the
largess of the wealthy rather than out of the earnings of
business. As a result, during the nineteenth century there
arose a group of private, nonsectarian charities supported and
administered by the new crop of middle-class philanthropists.

3. "Settlement" and "Charity Organization"

One of the precursors of the settlement movement in England, Edward Denison, recorded in his Journal on August 7,
1867, an account of the work done in East London, in which
can be identified a number of different functions, such as
adult education, public health, and social action, which later
became the concern of the settlement movement:

My opinion of the great sphere of usefulness to which I should
find myself admitted, by coming to live here is completely justi-
fied. All is yet in embryo—but it will grow. Just now I only teach
in a night school and do what in me lies in looking after the sick,
keeping an eye upon nuisances and the like, seeing that the local
authorities keep up to their work. I go tomorrow before the
Board at the workhouse, to compel the removal to the infirmary
of a man who ought to have been there already. I shall drive
the sanitary inspector to put the Act against overcrowding in
force, with regard to some houses in which there have been as
many as eight and ten bodies occupying one room. It is not surprising that the street in which this occurs has for months been
full of smallpox, scarlet fever and typhus. . . . These are the sort
of evils which, where there are no resident gentry, grow to a
height almost incredible, and on which the remedial influence of
the mere presence of a gentleman known to be on the alert is
inestimable.[4]

The settlement movement originated in England in a spirit
of religious service and philanthropy. The conditions in city

---

[4] Quoted in Woods and Kennedy, *The Settlement Horizon*, New York:
Russell Sage Foundation, 1922, p. 19. The author is indebted to Arthur
Dunham for pointing out the significance of this passage.

slums were pictured so vividly by Ruskin, Carlyle, and Kingsley that many university students became interested in the plight of the working class. A group of students at St. John's College, Cambridge, who wanted to do something for the poor and were not quite prepared to start a college mission, asked advice of the Rev. Canon Samuel A. Barnett. He suggested that they might rent a house in an industrial district where they could stay for short or long periods and learn to "sup sorrow with the poor." [5] This was the idea that led to the founding of the first settlement.

As shown later in some detail, groups of religiously motivated people sought to "settle" among "the poor" in the crowded cities, and to bring to them through friendly relations the advantages of the "better life," of which they had been deprived, and so to "uplift" them. The founders of the social settlement movement sought to know the neighborhood in which their neighbors lived and the conditions under which they lived. This prompted them to take action, and to help their neighbors to act, in order to improve the conditions of life.

"A settlement," says Werner Picht in *Toynbee Hall and the English Settlement Movement,* "is a colony of members of the upper classes, formed in a poor neighborhood, with the double purpose of getting to know the local conditions of life from personal observation, and of helping where help is needed. The settler gives up the comfort of a West End home, and becomes a friend of the poor. . . . The settler comes to the poor as man to man, in the conviction that it means a misfortune for all parties and a danger for the nation, if the different classes live in complete isolation of thought and environment. He comes to bridge the gulf between the classes." This "neighborhood work" became one of the characteristic features of the settlement.

[5] White, Gaylord S., "The Social Settlement After Twenty-Five Years." Reprinted from the *Harvard Theological Review,* IV, January, 1911, p. 1.

In their efforts to "organize" charity in the large cities of England, and later of the United States, in the latter part of the nineteenth century the "charity organization" societies endeavored to bring the giver and the receiver of the gift into personal contact through the voluntary friendly visitor for much the same reasons that the "settlement" people lived among "the poor." In the new cities the poor were crowded together in one neighborhood, the rich lived in another. It was hoped that by "settling" and "friendly visiting" the poor would absorb some of the culture and ideals of those from "better" neighborhoods. It was felt that a good moral effect on the poor would result from bringing them into contact with higher standards; this would also have a salutary effect on the rich by showing them the actual conditions under which the poor lived. This, it was hoped, would stir the consciences of those with culture and wealth. As in the case of the settlement movement the whole process was directed toward the amelioration of social conditions and attitudes that made for class conflict.

B. Charity Organization

1. *Philosophy*

The charity organization movement attempted to bring society's resources to bear on some of the social problems arising out of the conditions of the industrial revolution, by coordinating the work of the numerous relief societies and utilizing the method of friendly visiting. The particular forms of neighborhood organization used by the charity organization movement were adapted to the aims of the movement and the problems with which it dealt. Because this movement provided the basis for many later efforts in social welfare in which neighborhood organization was used it may be well to review briefly something of its basic social philosophy.

It was the industrial depression following 1873 which, in the United States, "afforded the starting-point for the examination and the reformation of the prevailing methods of charity." [6] Multitudes were thrown out of work. To these were added thousands of soldiers recently discharged from service in the Civil War. For the first time, unemployment became a national problem. Breadlines and soup kitchens appeared. Neglect and duplication resulted from the chaos of the numerous small, uncorrelated relief societies. One of the results was the extension of the charity organization movement.

According to the early philosophy of the charity organization movement the big problem was not poverty but "pauperism," which was regarded as a character defect. The character of the individual had to be improved through the influence of another individual upon him. Hence the great stress on neighborly intercourse with the poor. The "friendly visitors" were to prevent the poor from sinking into pauperism. The object of charity was to relieve those who were below what was called a line of "tolerable misery." Records of the time show the number of families "rescued from lives of chronic pauperism and started on respectable and self-dependent courses." [7] The prevention of pauperism was a major topic at the early meetings of the National Conference of Charities and Correction.

There was a great deal of apprehension lest pauperism endanger the social order, and the charity organization movement was sometimes supported for this reason. It was feared that "the poor, craving for human sympathy, yet feeling their moral deformity, should some fine day wreak their vengeance

[6] Kellogg, Charles D., "Charity Organization in the United States," *Proceedings of the National Conference of Charities and Correction, 1893*, Madison: Midland Publishing Co., 1893, pp. 53-54. This paper, together with *The Charity Organization Movement in the United States* by Frank D. Watson, New York: Macmillan Co., 1922, are liberally drawn upon in this section.

[7] Watson, Frank D., *The Charity Organization Movement in the United States*, New York: Macmillan Co., 1922, p. 217.

upon society at large." [8] The charity organization societies
were held to be the real answer to the socialistic and com-
munistic theories then being taught to the people with much
enthusiasm. It was thought that dealing directly with the
elements of character in concrete individual cases would
prove an antidote to those schemes which sought to improve
the conditions of men, without training them in how to
handle such situations. Charity organization leaders believed
they had the only sure way to reduce both poverty and
pauperism. [9]

During the industrial depression of 1893-1897 many of the
unemployed spurned "charity" and sought to do something
about the situation themselves. It was the era of Coxey's,
Kelly's, and other industrial armies. These protests focused
attention on the need to change social conditions. Some
leaders of the charity organization movement showed great
respect for the efforts on their own behalf made by the unemployed men and women. In an article on the "Unemployed"
the editor of *Lend-a-Hand* observed:

Labor demands justice, not charity, and this feeling kept over
9,000 families out of work who refused assistance. There was too
much truth in the belief that charity was a concession by wealth
to try and content labor with debasing poverty. The best systems
provided work for the unemployed. [10]

From an earlier issue we read:

[The winter] has shown very definitely, and to the immense
credit of all concerned, that the workingmen and women understand their own business exceedingly well—better than some of
the philanthropists. . . . The people who earn wages were, on

[8] *Ibid.*, p. 218. Quoted from Gurteen, S. Humphreys V., *Handbook of Charity Organization*, Buffalo: Published by the author, 1882.

[9] Brackett, Jeffrey R., "The Charity Organization Movement: Its Tendency and Its Duty," *Proceedings of the National Conference of Charities and Correction, 1895*, Boston: George H. Ellis, 1895, p. 86.

[10] Hale, E. E., ed., XIII, November, 1894, p. 6.

the whole, as well able to meet the storm as the people who earn salaries, or as those who live by cutting off coupons.[11]

The Reverend H. L. Wayland, founder of the Organized Charities Association of New Haven, suggested in 1886 that if employers gave to their employees that which was just and equal it would do away very largely with the need for "charity." He pointed out that the new ideas on charity do not suggest "that the employer should cut the laborer down below a living wage, and then give him a turkey at Christmas." [12]

At the International Congress of Charities, Correction, and Philanthropy in 1893, the point was made that in the largest cities pauperism could not be wisely considered alone. It was recognized that the problem of uplifting the general level of life had to be studied *as one whole problem,* especially as to the causes of existent evils. The question was asked whether the new charity organization movement had not been too long content to seek merely to relieve or "uplift" individuals "without asking if there are not prolific causes permanently at work to create want, vice, crime, disease, and death; and whether these causes may not be wholly or in large degree eradicated?" [13]

In looking at the period 1896-1904 in retrospect Watson observed that the outstanding characteristic was the emphasis charity organization societies placed upon prevention of poverty, as reflected in the various movements to change social conditions. There were nationwide campaigns for better housing, study and prevention of tuberculosis, and abolition of child labor. The dominant note of the period was a de-

[11] *Ibid.,* XII, January–June, 1894, p. 126.

[12] "The Old Charity and the New." An address delivered at the annual meeting of the New York Charity Organization Society in February, 1886. Quoted in Watson, *op. cit.,* p. 277.

[13] Paine, Robert Treat, Jr., "Pauperism in Great Cities: Its Four Chief Causes," *Proceedings of the International Congress of Charities, Correction, and Philanthropy, 1893,* Section I, pp. 25-35.

termination to seek and to eradicate those particular causes of dependency and the intolerable living conditions which were beyond the control of those whom they injured and destroyed.

The word "deserving" was dropping from the charity organization vocabulary. In discussing changes in charitable practices, Mary Richmond said in 1901: "In nothing does the change seem so marked as in our willingness to cooperate with the poor themselves and with their neighbors." [14]

2. District Organization

Many charity organization societies divided their cities into districts so that paid agents and volunteer friendly visitors would get to know the neighborhoods and the people in them more intimately. Within each district there were often several neighborhoods. The degree of autonomy they gave to district associations varied from city to city. There was also a great deal of variation in the form of district organization and the basis of districting.

One of the reasons for district organization was to make friendly visiting more effective. As noted earlier, the method of friendly visiting was developed in England. It was also developed in Germany in the 1850's. The Hamburg-Elberfeld system divided the city into "quarters," each unit containing not more than four dependent individuals or heads of families. The units were supervised by a visitor who called on the poor at regular intervals, kept informed of their circumstances, and used his influence to improve their manner of living. The quarters were grouped into districts, with a superintendent as the head of each. He arranged meetings of his visitors to discuss their work and decide on the amount, kind, and duration of aid to be given. There was a central administrative board over all the districts, which was re-

[14] Richmond, Mary E., "Some Methods of Charitable Cooperation II," *Charities*, VII, September 7, 1901, p. 197.

sponsible for their work and studied the causes of poverty. With the exception of the chairman of the central board all were volunteers. The advantage of this system was that the family developed an intimate relationship with the visitor. If relations became strained or if the visitor were incompetent this would be a disadvantage. Soon some volunteers became responsible for whole tenements. Later the system changed; larger territorial units were adopted, and the supervisors assigned visitors to cases.[15]

When the first charity organization society in America was organized in Buffalo in 1877, the city was divided into districts corresponding to the police precincts. District offices were opened in residences near the center of the district so that there would be no "taint of officialism" about the work, but that the poor might come to a real "home," with home surroundings and thus be, "perhaps unconsciously," bettered by the contact.[16] Watson saw this as the "settlement idea." It was never copied and was soon abandoned in Buffalo as it was too onerous for the paid agent.

The type of district organization which was developed in Philadelphia in 1878 sought to set up a complete charity organization society in each of the wards of the city. Twenty-three complete societies were formed in as many wards or groups of contiguous wards. Each raised its own relief funds and disbursed them without outer control. The Central Board met monthly and was composed of two delegates from each ward. The immediate results of this democratic but cumbersome scheme were that the Central Board itself became subordinate to the ward associations, and because the ward associations became so many new almsgiving societies, the older charitable societies refused to cooperate with them. In time the plan was revised so that the members of the Central Board were appointed, not by the ward associations,

---

[15] Queen, *op. cit.,* pp. 104-105.
[16] Gurteen, *op. cit.,* p. 127.

but by the annual meeting of the general society. The initiative and oversight of the Central Board were strengthened, and the wards were consolidated into 18 districts. The original plan, however, had made a deep impression which was not easily obliterated.[17]

Boston's experience was significant for the development of district organization. It demonstrated the value for each district of a district conference made up of three parts: (1) the district committee; (2) the representatives of various societies, and the officers, both public and private, working among the poor of the district; (3) the visitors. In Boston each district conference met weekly. Half an hour before the conference, the district committee met to look over the proposed business agenda and to dispose of such cases as did not require the attention of the district conference. This gave the society's agent an opportunity to ask questions and give advice, as well as serving to expedite the district conference which followed. The main function of the district committee was to know what resources were available. Each committee member was expected to know what services were offered by public departments and other sources for protection, shelter, relief, advice, transportation, loans, and the care of children.[18]

C. The Settlement

1. *The Settlement in the United States*

The settlement began as a center established by advantaged persons who desired to help the people of a deprived neighborhood, and developed rapidly into a significant social institution. As shown in later chapters, it has adapted itself to

[17] "Report of the Committee on History of Charity Organization," *Proceedings of the National Conference of Charities and Correction, 1893,* Madison: Midland Publishing Co., 1893, pp. 56-58.
[18] "Extracts from a Paper upon District Conferences" given by Mrs. James T. Fields of Boston. *New York Charity Organization Society Papers,* No. 3, May, 1882, pp. 1-2.

changing conditions and has continued in existence until the present day, making an important contribution to neighborhood organization for social welfare.

The first settlement in the United States, the Neighborhood Guild—later named University Settlement—was founded in New York City by Stanton Coit in 1886.[19] By 1897 there were 74 settlements in the United States, and by 1900 the number had increased to 103.[20]

According to Robert A. Woods, for many years headworker of South End House, Boston, the settlement assumed a special responsibility for all families living within the radius of a few blocks of the settlement house. It also sustained a general relation to the larger district encircling about the immediate neighborhood. It was concerned with developing institutional resources suited to the needs of a working-class community. This included relief of distress, removal of unsanitary conditions, care of neglected children, and recreation. Woods believed that an experiment of distinct importance to the American city was being worked out in the settlement method which he saw as an agency for social improvement. Although it was more costly than organized charity or popular education, he believed it was capable of solving an even more difficult and a more serious problem, namely, that of social integration. Alluding to William Booth's "submerged tenth" of the population, he said that the submerged type was easily "accessible" on the basis of its necessities and that the aristocracy of labor was accessible on the basis of its ambitions. Between these extremes, what Woods called the "class of labor" had the loyalties and passions of the proletariat. It scorned charity and was indifferent to offers of advanced education. The difficult task of the settlement was to study the complicated interplay of attachments that made up the

[19] White, *op. cit.*, p. 2.
[20] Woods, Robert A. and Kennedy, Albert J., *Handbook of Settlements*, New York: Charities Publication Committee, 1911, p. vi.

"consciousness of kind," felt by working people and to join with this group, as far as possible, in its struggle for a greater share of the fruits of civilization. To carry out its program of "social improvement" the settlement functioned as a "shaft" sent down to this stratum of society. As soon as the settlement worker became acquainted with representatives of the working class he was expected "to bring them into touch with men and women of the other classes, for the sake of friendly conference, and, if possible, for some form of practical cooperation." [21]

The settlement, said Woods, did not stand for relief or for instruction but rather for fellowship. One of the compensations accruing to the highly organized settlements was an opportunity to carry the settlement motive "up into education and down into charity." [22]

Woods maintained that the natural political following of the settlement was not the inhabitants of the neighborhood in which the settlement was located, but rather those public-spirited people throughout the city who shared the settlement philosophy and would support the settlement's actions in behalf of the masses of the people.

Jane Addams regarded the settlement as one manifestation of the attempt to "socialize democracy." Toward this end it conducted social and educational activities, so that the capitalist and the worker might meet as individuals beneath a friendly roof, open their minds to each other, and have their class theories "insensibly modified by the kindly attrition of a personal acquaintance." [23]

[21] Woods, Robert A., *The Neighborhood in Nation-Building*, New York: Houghton Mifflin Co., 1923, pp. 52-59.

[22] *Loc. cit.*

[23] Addams, Jane and others, *Philanthropy and Social Progress*, New York: Thomas Y. Crowell and Co., 1893, p. 54.

2. Cooperation of Settlements and Charity
Organization Societies

Although historically settlement work grew out of charity organization, residents of settlements were not always in sympathy with the prevailing methods of charity organization in the late nineteenth century. Many settlement workers considered their friendly contact with the people of their neighborhoods more effective for social betterment than the relief-giving activities of the charity organization societies. Both institutions used the neighborhood approach and their cooperation was essential to meet effectively the needs of people in the neighborhoods. It is noteworthy that when the Chicago Bureau of Charities attempted to deal with the depression of 1893-1897 the support given by the settlements was due to their desire to free themselves from the added pressure of relief work which was interfering with their own activities. This was the beginning of what later developed into greater recognition of the differences between settlements and charity organization societies, and of the value to each of the other's work.

As settlement and charity organization leaders studied their methods and purposes they found much ground in common. Speaking on "What Is Charity?" at the National Conference of Charities and Correction in 1896, Mary McDowell said that charity was undergoing a change at the hands of science. The settlement could not cooperate with charity if it were nothing more than a relief society, but could cooperate with it if charity offered a friendship that could change a life. The settlement could not stand idly by and ignore the physical needs of its neighbors. The problem of both the settlement and organized charity, she believed, was how to meet these needs in a way that would leave the neighbor on a higher spiritual plane. The settlement, she said, worked from within, while the charity organization society, with its voluntary friendly visitors and its paid agents, was the force coming from the outside into the neighborhood. They differed in method and yet complemented each other. Together they did what neither could completely do alone. She reported that a questionnaire sent to all the settlements in the country brought responses from 16 settlements, 15 of which said that they cooperated with the organized charities of their cities.

3. Mobilizing Neighborhood Forces

The early settlement leaders differed from one another not so much in goal as in method. They sought to identify and organize from within the neighborhood those forces through which the moral and material standards of living might be improved.

Robert Woods maintained that the real purpose of settlements was to re-establish those social relations which modern city life had thrown into confusion, and to develop such new forms of cooperative and public action as the changed situation might demand.[24] In the fifth annual report of South End House, dated December, 1896, there is an account of the close working relations maintained with other settlement houses, with the charity organization movement through representation on neighborhood conferences of the Associated Charities, and with other institutions. According to this report:

. . . it is the object of the settlement to establish in its own locality a synthesis of all available social forces; and in turn to supply local representation and support to all such forces in their larger operation.

The settlement itself does not act as a relief-giving center, but secures that end in a far better way by representation upon the local conferences of the Associated Charities. There are two delegates upon each of the neighboring conferences. Mr. Smallwood,

[24] Woods, Robert A., ed., The City Wilderness: A Settlement Study, Boston: Houghton Mifflin Co., 1898, pp. 248, 273-274. This is a study of the South End of Boston by residents of South End House. The section on "Social Recovery" was written by Robert A. Woods, Headworker.

from his long experience in such work, is able to give especially valuable aid. The House is represented upon the managing boards of various local institutions; such as, the Ward IX Day Nursery, the East Canton St. Dwellings (owned by the Cooperative Building Company), and the Wells Memorial Institute—all of which are in our own ward. Relations of constant friendly cooperation are kept up with Denison House on Tyler St. and with Lincoln House on Shawmut Ave. Our House supplies the local delegates to a variety of organizations that work throughout the city for better hygienic, political, economic, and moral conditions. . . .

The settlement is upon terms of cordial understanding and mutual helpfulness with the school teachers and the police officers of the neighborhood.[25]

Among the ideas on settlement work which Stanton Coit brought with him from England was a strong emphasis upon the innate forces of the neighborhood for "lifting the fallen classes of society into independence and prosperity." The fundamental idea was that "irrespective of religious belief or non-belief, all the people, men, women, and children, in any one street, or any small number of streets, in every working-class district" should be organized into a set of clubs, which by themselves, or together with those of other neighborhoods, could carry out all the reforms—"domestic, industrial, educational, provident, or recreative"—required by the social ideal. The Guild was not to limit itself to rescuing those who had already fallen into vice but was open to "wage earners" to prevent them from falling into these evils, and also to bring within their reach many advantages which they could not otherwise enjoy because they were beyond their individual means. Each neighborhood guild was to concentrate on the comparatively few persons living in its immediate vicinity—about 500 people.[26]

[25] *Fifth Yearly Report of the Settlement,* South End House Association, December, 1896, pp. 7-9.
[26] *Neighborhood Guilds: An Instrument of Social Reform,* London: Swan, Sonneschein and Co., 1891, pp. 1-11.

Coit attributed to Dr. Thomas Chalmers, the Scottish churchman, an appreciation of locality as a source of interest for philanthropic people. He said Chalmers also appreciated more than anyone else "the vast amount of help which was constantly being administered with wisdom and tenderness, in the poorest districts, by the neighbours themselves." Chalmers was so impressed with the worth and naturalness of such assistance that in bringing help to a family he often waited until the last possible moment, not so much to get the poor to care for the poorer as to give the spirit of neighborly responsibility the fullest opportunity to express itself. He organized his rich parishioners into disciplined bodies of workers, but never seemed to think of developing that "in-instinctive philanthropy" he found among the families of the "labouring classes." It was this latter idea, however, which Coit propounded as the root principle of the Neighborhood Guild.[27]

Coit believed that if the impulsive kindness of the poor were awakened to responsibility it would become a persistent principle of all-round care, one for another. He thought the poor as well as the rich needed education in their charity. If each neighborhood were organized in its own guild and if neighborhoods were united in those efforts which were too comprehensive for anyone to undertake alone, Coit predicted that the life of the entire city would be improved. And he doubted if this could be accomplished in any other way.

In the 1893 annual report of University Settlement in New York City we get some suggestion as to how Coit's ideas were to be put into practice. This report stated in part:

From the first it has been the idea of our Settlement that its residents shall only assist the working men and working women of this district themselves to carry on the educational, sanitary and other social reform movements that are needed here. . . . We must first bring into existence a local organization for social

[27] *Ibid.*, pp. 17-19.

reform; when we have done that, there will be little need of many volunteer workers from up-town; the most of the work will go on of itself as regards the outside public; only specialists need be called in. But it will take several years to build up a strong and wise local body of working people. Such an organization the Neighborhood Guild hopes to become . . . five clubs together (one of men and women, a second of young men, a third of young women, a fourth of boys, and the fifth for girls) will constitute the Neighborhood Guild. Each club will appoint delegates to the Central Guild Committee. This committee, on which three persons representing the University Settlement will also sit, will have charge of the Guild premises, and one member, at least, of the Guild Committee shall be on every special committee which undertakes any one branch of work, such as lecture courses, concerts, flower shows, anti-sweating work, etc.[28]

In this way Coit hoped to develop a self-directing organization of the people living within a neighborhood, an organization which would be able to raise the moral and material standards of life of the neighborhood.

Although differing with Coit in the matter of method, Woods sought an end result which was remarkably similar. Woods believed that when charity is administered by those who have struggled with poverty, when philanthropy works with those in its constituency instead of for them, when undertakings of demonstrated value for the general good flourish under either public or private auspices, then the local district will have progressed from the stage of "social recovery" and will have entered upon its normal, corporate growth.[29]

One of the first efforts to develop cooperation among settlements and other organizations with social welfare goals took place in Boston with the formal organization of the South End Social Union in 1899. Through the medium of this district-wide organization the eight philanthropic organizations represented in it conferred as to the best methods

[28] "Report and Plans for the Winter's Work," *University Settlement Society Bulletin*, November, 1893, pp. 10-11.
[29] Woods, ed., *The City Wilderness: A Settlement Study, op. cit.,* p. 287.

of work and how to avoid overlapping of their work in the neighborhoods. It was a channel for united action on issues involving public health and public order. It conducted such adult education activities as lectures, picture shows, and concerts, and called public meetings on matters of concern to the district. It appeared before the city government and the state legislature on behalf of the district.[30] Out of this beginning a city-wide organization, the Boston Social Union, was formed a few years later.

In summary, the charity organization societies and settlements of this period, in order to achieve their purposes, developed forms of neighborhood organization suitably adapted to their methods. As will be seen in the next chapter the neighborhood approach continued to be used in these and succeeding social welfare movements.

[30] *South End Association, Eighth Annual Report,* Boston: January, 1900, p. 15.

CHAPTER II

BEGINNINGS OF THE COMMUNITY
ORGANIZATION MOVEMENT

A. Background: 1900 to World War I

1. *Social Conditions*

The financial panic of 1907 had been preceded by ten years of extraordinary economic prosperity. It was followed by a depression that extended through the winter and brought a phenomenal increase in the number of unemployed. Many new charity organization societies were established. They set up employment exchanges and took a leading part in mobilizing the resources of their communities to meet emergency relief needs. To make ends meet many families made adjustments that lowered living standards to such an extent that harmful aftereffects were suffered. Some lost their homes and had to move to furnished rooms. Others rented out rooms, took in boarders, or sold some of their furniture. Many had to live on wages from part-time work. The economic effects of this depression were felt until 1910.

A large number of movements arose to ameliorate the evil effects of these conditions. Mary Richmond reported at the

National Conference of Charities and Correction in 1910 that more social movements of national scope had been organized between 1900 and 1910 than all existing similar movements organized before that date. Of 39 national health and welfare organizations launched in this period the distribution was as follows: public health, eight; welfare of children, seven; church social services, seven; social service in general, five; protection of industrial workers, four; education, three; prison reform, two; city problems, two; protection of the immigrant, one.[1]

In this period, the coordination of the activities of various agencies concerned with social disorganization together with the recognition of the "community" as an entity combined to create the community organization movement. As shown below, this movement was a successor to some aspects of charity organization already established. As a movement for social welfare its concern for "community" extended from neighborhood to nation.

The depression of 1914-1915 brought a winter of distress surpassing that of 1907-1908. To a degree previously unknown, unemployment was regarded as a community responsibility and the remedy recommended for it was *work*. Charity organization societies had developed plans to meet the crisis. They relied mainly upon city governments and industry to provide jobs; when these resources were inadequate, they stimulated and cooperated in other efforts to secure real work. With the advent of World War I industry reabsorbed many of the unemployed to fill orders for war materials.

2. Social Surveys

In the late nineties muckraking was the method used to bring undesirable social conditions to the attention of the

[1] *Proceedings of the National Conference of Charities and Correction, 1910,* Fort Wayne: National Conference of Charities and Correction, 1910, p. 212.

public for action. At the turn of the century this was being replaced by an emphasis on fact-finding social surveys.

One of the earliest of these was the study of Washington, D. C. made in 1905, which resulted in a report showing the evil conditions that existed in the very shadow of the White House. This survey had been inaugurated by the editorial staff of *Charities and Commons,* a magazine of national scope published by the Charities Publication Committee of the New York Charity Organization Society. When the Russell Sage Foundation was organized in 1907 one of its first acts was to grant funds to finance the Pittsburgh Survey which has since become the classic example of the social survey method.

The Pittsburgh Survey attempted a social and economic "diagnosis" of an American industrial district. It sought to study conditions under which people lived and worked in a great industrial city, and was concerned with civic conditions as well as with industrial relations. Included within its scope were sanitation, public health, dependency, assimilation of nationality groups and minorities, wages, hours, and the organization of labor. Some practical steps were looked for which the whole community could agree were necessary. Appropriate legislation was hoped for, based on standards that were accepted and that were in line with conventional procedure. It was felt that this would provide material on the basis of which social conditions all over the United States could be understood.

When the field work ended in 1908 the two things the investigating staff saw most clearly as problems demanding attention were: (1) the twelve hour day, and (2) social neglect. As the investigating staff said:

Certainly no community before in America or Europe has ever had such a surplus, and never before has a great community applied what it had so meagerly to the rational purposes of human life. Not by gifts of libraries, galleries, technical schools, and parks, but by the cessation of toil one day in seven and sixteen hours in the twenty-four, by the increase of wages, by the sparing of lives, by the prevention of accidents, and by raising the standards of domestic life, should the surplus come back to the people of the community in which it is created.[2]

Following this survey, the Pittsburgh method of studying a community's social problems came into widespread use. When the Russell Sage Foundation established a Department of Surveys and Exhibits in 1912 it was almost immediately flooded with requests for social surveys in various cities. Just prior to the outbreak of World War I such national organizations as the American Association for Organizing Family Social Work, the American Red Cross, the National Child Labor Committee, and the Federal Children's Bureau were conducting surveys as a regular part of their programs. *Charities and Commons* changed its name to *The Survey* in the hope that this title would signify the definite, positive, and constructive purposes for which the Pittsburgh Survey stood.

The early promoters of the survey movement were social workers and others interested in community betterment. As a result, the making of a survey consisted not only in description of conditions but also included setting forth recommendations and working out plans for their implementation as a part of the program of community improvement. Thus this early method of community study can be said to have provided essential groundwork for the community organization movement. As a matter of fact, without the methods developed by the survey movement the community organization field would not have flourished as it did.[3]

[2] Devine, Edward T., "Pittsburgh the Year of the Survey," *The Pittsburgh Survey* (Volume on the Pittsburgh District, Civic Frontage), New York: Survey Associates, 1914, p. 4.

[3] Steiner, Jesse F., *Community Organization*, New York: Century, 1925, p. 194.

3. *Neighborhood and Community Organization*

It should not be surprising to find beginnings of the community organization movement in the charity organization, school center (discussed below), and settlement movements of this period. These movements were concerned not only with neighborhoods but with larger communities.

The city-wide central council of social agencies developed as a direct result of the efforts of the charity organization society to coordinate social services. The financial federation, which had originated earlier, also developed at this time. These organizations were concerned with coordination, planning, and financing at the city-wide level. The charity organization society, however, continued to strengthen its district committees and to stimulate the organization of citizens in the neighborhoods.

It was during the first decade of the century that the school center movement arose. The "school civic center" was an attempt to get more citizens to participate in civic affairs. It was hoped that through organizations of citizens formed around the school civic centers there would be a revival of integrated neighborhood life. As the movement progressed, however, the recreational aspects of the program proved far more popular than the civic and cultural aspects. Many felt that the school should also be the center of the social life of the neighborhood and so the term "school social center" came into vogue. With the development of the "community organization movement" the school centers became known more and more as "community centers." As will be shown below, leaders of this movement were convinced that the social disorganization of our large cities could be successfully combated by widespread organization of such centers. In what follows, the term "school center" will be used to refer to these developments.

Through its experienced personnel the settlement made

an important contribution to the school center movement. Nevertheless, settlement workers criticized this movement because of the lack of intimate personal contact between the staff and the neighborhood. This recognition by the settlements of the need for better methods of working with people was an important stimulus to the later development of social group work.

The settlement movement in this period of the early 1900's continued to organize neighborhood groups of citizens and also began to develop city-wide federations of settlements.

Neighborhood organization was given a powerful impetus during World War I when the school center movement was used as the starting point for organizing defense councils.

B. Charity Organization

1. *Family and Neighborhood*

As we saw in Chapter I, charity organization developed district committees so that its paid agents and voluntary friendly visitors might become acquainted with the conditions of neighborhood life. From its experience in having brought together many individuals and agencies interested in the "treatment of distress" the charity organization movement found that individuals and families could not be considered apart from their community relations.

This was indicated in Mary Richmond's list of forces with which the charity worker might cooperate: family forces, personal forces, neighborhood forces, civic forces, private charitable forces, public relief forces. The problem of charity in the case of a family asking for aid was to get them from "private charitable forces" to "family forces" by utilizing all the forces that lay in between.[4]

[4] Richmond, Mary E., "Some Methods of Charitable Cooperation I," *Charities*, VII, May, 1901, pp. 108-110.

Mary Richmond maintained that a wise use of neighborhood forces was the basis of success in the district plan adopted by the larger charity organization societies. The district, in addition to being a more manageable unit, made possible a spirit of neighborliness which charity organization leaders considered to be a large element in all true charity. The district agent and the district committee familiar with the normal life of the district knew how to deal with its abnormal conditions.

The neighborly spirit of cooperation and self-help was developed still further through the use of the district office as a meeting place for all interested in the social needs of the neighborhood. Certain districts of the New York Charity Organization Society were instrumental in organizing neighborhood associations. These were not organically connected with the district committees of the Society but many of the same people were interested in each. Local initiative in the neighborhood associations organized by the Society existed within a framework in which control was centralized.

2. *District Committees*

The organization and function of the district committees of the New York Charity Organization Society is described in the Society's Twenty-fifth Annual Report, published in 1907. The standing committees of the Central Council were appointed by the president after each annual election. One of them, a Committee on District Work, was related to the district committees in the same way as the Executive Committee was related to standing committees. There were ten district committees, one in each of the sections into which the city was divided for the society's purposes. The district committees were responsible within their respective areas for the care of needy families in their own homes. The original members of the district committees were appointed by the Central

Council. After that, each committee became self-perpetuating, and, subject to the approval of the Council, it made its own choices of persons to fill vacancies. As the report says:

It is the function of the district committees to "manage the work of the Society" within their own boundaries, "subject to the control of the Council." They "establish" the district offices; decide on the treatment of the cases applying for assistance in their part of the city; carry the responsibility for developing cooperation with the Society by churches, other charitable agencies, and residents of the district; and take part, more or less actively as their interests lead them, in carrying on the general educational work of the Society. They have no responsibility, as committees, in raising money for their expenses. The finances of the society have been centralized from the beginning. The paid employees for the district work are appointed by authority of the Central Council, subject to the approval of the district committee to which they are assigned.[5]

From this description we see that the Central Council retained administrative control over its operating units in the districts. In the example of the previous period, cited in Chapter I, ultimate control rested for a time in the district organizations; this tended to make each of these a separate charity organization society and to make the administration of uniform policies difficult.

Guides to the internal organization and function of a district committee were set forth in a pamphlet on *The Wheels of Organized Charity: The Work of a District Committee,* published in 1909 by the Buffalo Charity Organization Society for its ten district committees. District committees, it said, should be representative of all the interests which affect dependent families in any way. They should include friendly visitors, a lawyer, a doctor, a nurse (ready to do special work for the district committee on request), representatives of charities working in the district, and a few intelligent, resourceful persons with special knowledge of conditions and life in the district. The function of the district committee included both the working out and the deciding upon of plans for the treatment of families, and then supervising the execution of these plans. The committee was also to survey the charitable fields to keep in touch with movements for the prevention of poverty, and be informed about improved methods for dealing with dependent families, so that any family coming before the committee would receive the best possible care. In this way also the social outlook of committee members was broadened so that on the basis of their experience with individual dependent families they might better understand the need for larger programs of social improvement. The district committee was also responsible for promoting movements for the improvement of bad social conditions in the district.[6]

3. Councils of Social Agencies

As the charity organization movement developed the leaders of the social movements in each of a number of cities came together to form a federation through which to plan a city's social development. According to Francis McLean, this had its basis in the two fundamental principles of charity organization, namely, "case-by-case work and cooperation, which, of course, naturally leads on to prevention." Certain responsibilities grew out of these principles. The charity organization movement had to grasp the problem not only of social welfare, but of coordination in social welfare for the betterment of social conditions.[7]

McLean said that during the first two years of field work

[6] The Wheels of Organized Charity: The Work of a District Committee, Buffalo: Charity Organization Society, 1909, pp. 1-4.
[7] McLean, Francis H., Charity Organization Field Work, New York: Russell Sage Foundation, 1910, pp. 18-19. This source is also drawn upon for much of the discussion immediately following.

on a national scale in the charity organization movement, the organization secretaries attempted to become more adequately informed on relations between affiliated organizations and on the social problems of a city, even though the major concern of the charity organization society might be that of "an educator of public opinions." Some of the older societies sponsored conferences to stimulate broader cooperation. These conferences did not result in coordinated planning but served as an educational medium for movements in this direction. The conception of an organization for social planning emerged gradually from situations involving intersociety relations and as the accumulative result of various field work activities. The central council of philanthropies or social agencies became the channel through which social agencies could take joint action for social reforms, bring their influence to bear on particular situations in the community, or encourage the development of new societies whenever these were required. Although councils often began at the city-wide level they developed forms of neighborhood and district organization. This development will be discussed later, pp. 115-122.

The first manual describing the methods and purposes of the council of social agencies was published by the American Association for Organizing Family Social Work in 1920. This name was later adopted by the American Association for Organizing Charity.

4. *Family Social Work*

In 1919 the American Association for Organizing Charity adopted the policy that the family rather than the community should be regarded as the peculiar unit of charity organization. It was suggested that the words "family social work" be incorporated in the titles of local agencies. In line with the trend indicated by this report charity organization societies were becoming more explicitly direct service agencies. The coordinating function previously carried by the central council of the charity organization society now became the function of the independent council of social agencies.

Since their inception charity organization societies had been faced with the conflict between offering direct service to individuals and families and at the same time coordinating their efforts with those of the other direct-service agencies. The decision that the family rather than the community was to be the particular unit of charity organization marked the separation of family social work from community organization. This left each movement free to develop its own methods for tackling the same basic human problems.

The family welfare associations continued to carry on many community activities in connection with such matters as housing reform, juvenile courts, marriage laws and were instrumental in organizing social service exchanges. They developed children's departments, legal aid bureaus, anti-tuberculosis work, and public health services. Many of these services later became the functions of separate agencies.

C. Settlements

1. *Growth of the Settlement Movement*

The settlements gradually won recognition for themselves as agencies and recognition of the neighborhood as a significant grouping of people in urban areas. At the National Conference of Charities and Correction in 1902 there was for the first time a section devoted to neighborhood work.

In this period there was a rapid increase in the number of settlements. As noted in Chapter I there were 103 settlements in 1900. In the succeeding five years the number almost doubled, and between 1905 and 1911 the number doubled again so that by 1911 there were 413 settlements in the United States.[8]

[8] Woods, Robert A. and Kennedy, Albert J., *Handbook of Settlements,* New York: Charities Publication Committee, 1911, p. vi.

During the period here under review, the settlements provided leadership in the establishment of playgrounds for children and recreation facilities for adults. The settlements were a powerful influence in supplementing the wider activities of the public schools. They demonstrated how educational facilities could be extended to include the adults of a community. They were influential in raising standards of sanitation and hygiene, and they fostered interest in public health. South End House in Boston, Hull House in Chicago, and Henry Street Settlement in New York City were prominent in these activities.

One of the interesting developments of this period took place in Los Angeles where six municipal settlements were set up. These were playgrounds offering a variety of services —club activities, dances, entertainments, branch libraries, and home nursing. Each settlement was managed by a man and a woman assistant. A residence on the playground was furnished for the director and his family. Volunteers aided the paid staff.

A tribute to the effectiveness of settlement initiative was the erection of neighborhood-center buildings in each of twelve small parks in Chicago, at a cost of $90,000 each. Small groups of settlement workers located themselves near such public buildings where they sought to render service to the community.

2. Forerunners of the Community Organization Movement

In the opinion of Jesse F. Steiner the settlements were the forerunners of the modern "community movement." As shown above, they did not bring about a correlation of agencies in the community, but rather established a neighborhood center where the best representatives of education and culture could meet with those who did not have these advantages on terms of neighborly intimacy.

The point of view of the settlement worker continued to

be different from that of the teacher, the charity worker, the mission worker, and the student of social research because his knowledge of the neighborhood was not regarded as limited or qualified by any special interest beyond that of becoming acquainted with his neighbors, knowing the facts about their struggles and aspirations, and the conditions under which they worked and lived. Since the settlement worker did not "profess" anything, he was not met "by that defensive attitude on the part of his neighbors which the visit of the professional worker calls out." [9]

It was to the settlement worker that workers in other agencies looked for knowledge of neighborhoods and districts. Homer Folks, writing in 1902, expressed the belief that the settlement worker should be able to report on such matters as: which agencies shape opinion in any particular district, what forces count most in the assimilation of the foreign population, and why the preacher has so little influence and the district political leader so much. The settlement, he felt, might exert its influence in a manner similar to the political leader.[10]

The leadership role of the settlement in the neighborhood continued to be a dual one. At the sixth annual meeting of the National Federation of Settlements in New York City, in 1916, Mary Simkhovitch stated that the settlements realized that although it was their duty to stimulate social reforms and carry these into effect, a more fundamental task was to release the dormant powers of the neighborhoods themselves. It was towards this end that the Chicago Commons sponsored its Men's Community Club. As outlined in an article in *The Commons:*

The members of the Municipal Club and the Neighborhood League have united to form one strong social and civic organiza-

[9] White, Gaylord S., "The Social Settlement After Twenty-five Years." Reprinted from the *Harvard Theological Review*, IV, January, 1911, p. 11.
[10] Folks, Homer, "Functions of a Social Settlement," *Charities*, VIII, May, 1902, pp. 481-482.

tion, which has most auspiciously entered upon a career of wide
influence and usefulness under the name of "The Community
Club in the 17th Ward." Its object is "to foster personal fellowship, to promote the cause of social unity, to inspire civic patriot-
ism and encourage co-operation for the betterment of municipal
conditions." To its membership, which includes at the start 75
men, "any male resident of this community above the age of
twenty years may be eligible." The Club is to be strictly non-
partisan and non-sectarian. At the initial banquet, which was
beautifully served by the Chicago Commons Woman's Club,
prominent representatives of different nationalities, parties and
faiths vied with each other in appreciative tributes to the value
of the common ground and unifying spirit furnished by the
settlement.[11]

An account of the South End Improvement Society of Boston exemplifies the activity of a settlement fostering an improvement association through which the people of the district could bring about social reforms. Formed in 1908, the
Society in one year had a paying membership of 500. It was
established to develop public spirit in an area where such
spirit had almost entirely disappeared. Regular removal of
ashes and garbage was instituted as a result of the Society's
criticism of Boston's sanitation. The organization secured
a thousand signatures in favor of an antismoke nuisance
measure then before the state legislature. Its plans included
a general public health campaign for the South End. The
executive secretary, a resident of South End House, devoted a
considerable portion of his time to the work of the Society.
He and Robert A. Woods were delegates to the United Improvement Association, a federation of 16 district improvement societies throughout Boston.

Hudson Guild, a New York settlement, sought to follow
Stanton Coit's principles and stressed the participation of the
people of the neighborhood. The Guild House was regarded
simply as the center of an association which extended
throughout the district where most of the members of the

[11] *The Commons*, VI, May, 1901, p. 15.

clubs lived. The governing body of the House was the Council, to which each of the evening clubs elected delegates. The president of the Council was ex officio a member of the Board of Trustees. Working through several committees, the Council met monthly and dealt with all matters pertaining to the welfare of the Guild.

A District Committee was set up consisting of a man and a woman from each block. They were asked to serve as captains of their immediate vicinity. The women were to look after sick babies, cases of extreme poverty and distress, and similar matters that came to their attention. The men were to report on violations of the health laws and disorderly saloons, as well as the gangs that made the district unwholesome for family life. The chairman of the District Committee, who functioned as the executive of the Committee, was in constant touch with the Health Department, the Tenement House Department, and the police captains of the adjoining precincts. Committee members often came from families that had been helped and were in turn eager to help someone else. It was pointed out to those who benefited from this help that they were under obligation to help other people by reporting cases of sickness or destitution to the Guild, and if possible by doing something themselves. In brief, the District Committee sought to make the people of the district aware of their common interests so that they themselves could bring about better conditions.

3. Settlement Federations

In addition to fostering groups of neighborhood residents that worked together with other organizations, the settlements formed federations of settlements. The Boston Social Union, referred to in Chapter I, was one of the first. It was founded in 1908 by representatives of the South End Social Union, and the Social Union of the North and West Ends. It had its own office and a paid assistant secretary. Its purpose was to unite the activities of all the settlements and neighborhood houses in the city for broader and more effective service. Sixteen settlements were thus brought together, all of them nonsectarian. Meetings were called to eliminate overlapping and competition of settlement workers in specialized fields; meetings of athletic leaders, teachers of cooking, and so forth were initiated. There was talk of forming district associations. One function given important consideration was that of how to further movements for the extension to the whole city of needed services whose value had been demonstrated in one neighborhood. It kept its members informed of the best developments in the social services and sought to involve citizens who were members of the local settlements in broader activity.

It was suggested that by working together with federations in other large cities and with state federations a foundation would be created for a national organization of "local social workers." Such a federation was expected to provide a channel for dealing with settlement problems of national scope; it was not to confine itself to discussions of individual local problems. Out of those beginnings the National Federation of Settlements was organized in 1911.

D. School Centers

1. *The School as Center of Neighborhood Life*

Eleanor T. Glueck in her study of the schoolhouse as an instrument for the organization of neighborhood life contended, not that the school was the best neighborhood center in every neighborhood, but rather that insofar as a nation-wide program was concerned for the purposeful organization of neighborhood life, it was the most suitable center. She pointed out that it was public property, nonsectarian, non-partisan, nonexclusive, and widespread in its influence upon the life of the people through their children. As mentioned earlier, the leaders of the school center movement were convinced that school centers could help effectively in combating social disorganization in our large cities.

One of the earliest experiments in publicly supported school centers took place in Rochester. In 1907 the School Extension Committee, representing 11 organizations, got an appropriation of $5,000 from the Board of Education and inaugurated the practice of using school buildings for civic and social purposes to attract both adults and young persons.[12] The organizations were: Central Trade and Labor Council, Playground League, College Women's Club, Daughters of the American Revolution, Humane Society, Labor Lyceum, Local Council of Women, Officers' Association of Mothers' Clubs, Political Equality Club, Social Settlement Association, and Women's Educational and Industrial Union.

The school board selected Edward J. Ward as civic secretary to supervise this wider use of the school plant. An experiment was conducted in one school in the center of the city in a "middle-class neighborhood." It was initiated by a general neighborhood gathering addressed by the president of the Board of Education, who explained the basic idea of the school center as an institute through which the community might serve itself. For the second year the appropriation was $10,000. Sixteen schools were used as neighborhood clubhouses, and a city-wide federation of civic clubs was formed in which each school center was represented. The appropriation for the third year was $20,000. However, the ward bosses were opposed to the project and prevented its further development when they won out at the next election.

The Rochester experiment created wide interest; it stimulated discussion by the National Municipal League, the Playground Association of America, the National Education Association, and in teachers' institutes.

[12] Glueck, Eleanor T., *Community Use of Schools*, Baltimore: Williams and Wilkins, 1927, pp. 18-19.

Edward J. Ward conceived of the school center as the capital of the precinct. He contended that the school should be the polling place and the place for discussion of community problems, and that it should have a Voters' League to unite people for civic improvement. It should be a recreational and cultural center offering public lecture courses, public art exhibitions and music programs, and a branch public library. It should be an employment center and contain a branch of the health board. Above all, it should be a place where all the people of the community could become acquainted. According to Mrs. Glueck, the development between 1909 and 1910 of school centers in several cities showed that Ward's idea for a school center was a composite of ideas from a number of centers rather than a blueprint for any specific center.[13]

In 1909 Ward was invited by the Extension Department, University of Wisconsin, to organize school centers throughout Wisconsin. The Wisconsin Bureau of Civic and Social Center Development was set up. It provided an adviser for local communities and consultation services. In October, 1911, it called the First National Conference on Civic and Social Center Development "to promote the development of intelligent public spirit through community use of the common schoolhouse for free discussion of public questions and all wholesome civic, educational, and recreational activities.[14] Two distinct types of school centers were discernible in the deliberations: (1) highly standardized and paternal, and (2) the spontaneous and democratic kind which Ward had established in Rochester. The conference was characterized by an almost religious enthusiasm and marked the beginning of the school center movement on a large scale.

During the campaign which resulted in the election of

[13] *Ibid.*, pp. 21-22. See study made by Perry, Clarence A., *Evening Recreation Centers*, New York: Russell Sage Foundation, 1910.
[14] Glueck, *op. cit.*, p. 25.

Woodrow Wilson to the Presidency, the issue was raised as to whether the polling places should be shifted to the schoolhouses, which were then to become the deliberative as well as the voting headquarters of district political organizations. The "social center idea" was endorsed by the leaders of the political parties, by the National Education Association, and similar bodies. This new concept was accompanied by the beginning of social center development in so many communities throughout the country that Ward believed intelligent self-expression to be assured.

The change from the paternalistic center to one that had a self-governing committee, consisting of one representative from each member club of the center, was due largely to the influence of the People's Institute of New York. Since about 1913 the Brooklyn People's Institute had been helping communities in Brooklyn to form their own neighborhood organizations. They met in schools and had no restrictions of race, creed, or political affiliation. A community center was not defined as a building or as a set of activities, but rather as an organizing center for the life of the neighborhood. The public school was regarded as the natural place for the community center for practical reasons, since school buildings were found in all neighborhoods and were used only half the time. There were equally important reasons of principle, since the school belonged to the public and was the most important agency of the state for spreading knowledge and fostering civic ideals. The community center worker was regarded as a neighborhood leader; he was on the job continuously; he stimulated the community to develop its own activities, and he showed how they could pay their way. The successful community center, it was believed, required full-time leaders or their equivalent.

A good example of successful leadership was Clinton S. Childs who developed the community center in Public School

63 in New York City. He lived in the neighborhood and spent almost two months there before any activities were instituted. According to the Social Center Committee of the People's Institute:

. . . Three-fourths of his work was done outside the school building. He discovered the potential leadership of his neighborhood and organized a governing committee, himself acting as chairman of this committee. He sought to know the wishes of the people. He was acquainted with all the dance halls, the motion-picture shows, even the saloon influences of his district. He brought conscious social art to bear, in the planning of activities and the choice and guidance of voluntary help. . . .[15]

The work at Public School 63 in New York City began to attract attention. The center was open not only to young people of both sexes, but was patronized by many adults as well. Local businessmen and women helped in the arrangement of programs for the young people of the district. Social workers came from all over the city to visit the center. It was hoped that a formula had been discovered by which all the schools of the city could be converted into centers of community life without a proportionate increase in taxes. Clinton S. Childs epitomized the dream as follows:

A Community clubhouse and Acropolis in one; this is the Social Center. A community organized about some center for its own political and social welfare and expression; to peer into its own mind and life, to discover its own social needs and then to meet them, whether they concern the political field, the field of health, of recreation, of education or of industry; such community organization is necessary if democratic society is to succeed and endure. There must be an unifying social bond of feeling, tradition, experience, belief, and knowledge, a common meeting ground, spiritually and concretely speaking. But there must also

[15] *Notes on Community Center Work in School Buildings,* New York: Social Center Committee of the People's Institute, Pamphlet No. 1, March, 1915, pp. 5-6.

be a community expression through activity, self-government, and self-support.[16]

2. *School Centers and Settlements*

Eleanor T. Glueck considered the settlement impractical as the medium for a nationwide program for preserving the neighborhood unit because it was privately financed. Nevertheless, the technique of neighborhood organization and the method of education and integration of community forces had to be borrowed from the settlement.

It was the settlement movement that first realized the need for an institution through which neighborhood consciousness could be preserved, strengthened, and directed toward individual and group welfare. The programs of the settlement were designed to bring into harmony the many sectarian, racial, and social groups of a neighborhood.

One of the questions settlement workers had to answer was: How far do school and community centers, and various local agencies of other sorts, take the place of the settlement, and what is the future of the settlement in the light of what they are undertaking? In answer to this question Robert A. Woods reported in 1921 that about 170 cities including New York, Chicago, Pittsburgh, Buffalo, Detroit, and Minneapolis had established school centers, either directly or indirectly under the auspices of the municipality. At least 25 per cent of the school centers were actually conducted by private agencies. These centers did not differ much from those conducted by the settlements and, according to Woods, they were among the best.

In a fair proportion of cases district improvement societies or community councils had a more or less responsible relation to the school center. In many well-to-do communities

[16] In Perry, Clarence A. and Williams, Marguerita P., *New York School Centers and their Community Policy,* New York: Russell Sage Foundation, 1931, pp. 26-27. Quoted from Childs, Clinton S., *A Year's Experiment in Social Center Organization,* New York: People's Institute, 1913.

considerable responsibility was assumed by local residents. In less-favored communities local collective action was frequently aroused and led by outsiders. This pattern differed very little from that of many settlements where settlement residents took the lead in neighborhood improvement associations that sometimes met in school buildings.

School centers could provide education for citizenship, large-scale education and recreation, and a local public headquarters for all citizens in matters of local civic activities. They did not, however, cover as great a variety of interests as did the settlements; nor were the relations with club leaders as close. They drew from a larger area than the settlements and generally found their best constituency in districts removed from the center of the city. Settlements concentrated on the neighborhood and believed less resourceful districts needed more than the school centers offered.

Teachers in the school came from outside the neighborhood and did not have a close relationship with its people. Building up a local agency for community betterment implied responsible groups representing local interest to see that plans were carried through and programs maintained. In Chicago, where the playgrounds provided elaborate social centers the year round, the need for resident workers was felt. Los Angeles, as mentioned earlier, actually established settlement houses in connection with playground centers. Several members of the Boston Social Union had long-since established successful neighborhood centers under private initiative. These centers added resident groups of workers according to the settlement plan.

The settlements witnessed the failure of many attempts at local community organization, which Woods attributed to the lack of enlightened and determined leadership. The settlements trained workers, not only for themselves, but for other organizations as well. In Woods' opinion the community center needed "a small capable group, held in some spe-

cial fellowship, having some sort of intimate corporate base
for this fellowship, and living individually and collectively as
hospitable neighbors among the people." [17] Thus the community center could carry over the "inner essence" of the
settlement.

With World War I came a wider interest in neighborhood
and community organization. Instead of social settlements in
"slum" districts the community organization movement came
to emphasize more and more "the self-organization of natural
groupings of people." [18] The school centers as well as the
district improvement societies usually did not have so wide a
range of services as the settlements, nor did they place so
much emphasis upon family and neighborhood affairs. However, as Woods pointed out at the National Conference of
Social Work in 1917, the widest dissemination of the spirit
of the settlement was done not by the settlement itself so
much as through the newer developments which to a large
extent grew out of it.

In the years immediately preceding World War I the school
center movement spread rapidly. In 1911 there were 248
school buildings being used for community purposes in 48
cities. By 1913 the numbers had increased to 629 school buildings in 152 cities. One of the factors influencing this development was the Conference on Civic and Social Center Development held in Madison, Wisconsin in 1911. The National
Community Center Association was organized as an outgrowth of this conference.[19]

In summary, a shift of emphasis occurred in this period
from neighborhood organization covering a geographic area
with a program of service to people in need, to neighborhood

[17] Woods, Robert A., *The Neighborhood in Nation-Building*, Boston and
New York: Houghton Mifflin Co., 1923, p. 319.
[18] Glueck, *op. cit.*, p. 28.
[19] In 1924 the Association was absorbed into the National Education Association. Its publication *The Community Center* was merged with *Social Forces*
in which it had a special section.

organization as part of a movement to revitalize communities. There was also a dawning recognition of the fact that co-ordinating the efforts of a number of direct-service agencies cannot be accomplished by an agency which itself offers a program of direct service. This point gains in significance in later periods.

CHAPTER III

THE COMMUNITY ORGANIZATION MOVEMENT

A. Background: World War I to 1929

1. *"Back to Normalcy"*

Following the wartime production boom came a postwar depression, and its accompanying unemployment. By the early twenties the country was pulling out of this depression, and the national slogan had become "Back to Normalcy." In 1929 the pendulum was to swing from a period of unprecedented economic prosperity to the beginning of another depression. The poverty, vice, congestion, and class conflict that had persistently accompanied the industrial revolution became even more pronounced.

Some medium was needed to counteract these effects and to coordinate the various efforts to alleviate distress and to ameliorate conditions. During the war, as already noted, local community ties had been mobilized by the defense councils to support the war effort. When the war was over, there was great hope that this method of mobilizing neighborhood community forces might prove an effective means of solving the problems of peace.

2. *The Neighborhood Community*

As mentioned earlier, the "community movement" sought to establish in urban neighborhoods the intimacy of village life.[1] There was much criticism of this movement. Many sociologists were of the opinion that the local community as a unit of social organization was booked for discard. They pointed out that although formerly the local group had been a powerful influence in regulating behavior, community consciousness in the large city was weak and vague. Reawakening of this consciousness was considered a very difficult task. These sociologists decried the efforts of the social workers who were trying to revive simple group life through the organization of a city into blocks, neighborhoods, and communities. Social settlements, community centers, and similar devices were not effective enough to prevent the disintegration of the neighborhood. Impressed by the reduction in the significance of distance brought about by the automobile, the world-wide news services, and the radio, they sought to reconcile themselves to a scheme of life in which there could be little of the neighborly New England town-meeting kind of association.[2]

There was on the other hand considerable support for the view that the impetus toward neighborhood life was still strong. Granted that there were forces and interests that inevitably carried people beyond their immediate vicinity, there was at the same time a strengthening of neighborhood ties in the typical development of neighborhood chain stores, movies, decentralized public libraries, and recreation facilities. Also, the transportation systems that had made possible

[1] For an account of the development of the "community movement" see Steiner, Jesse F., "An Appraisal of the Community Movement," *Journal of Social Forces*, VII, March, 1929, pp. 334 ff.

[2] Queen, Stuart A., *Social Work in the Light of History*, Philadelphia: J. B. Lippincott, 1922, p. 320.

the growth of large cities had become enormously complicated; this drove the neighborhood back into itself. There
was, however, some recognition of the interdependence
among the various parts of a city. The danger of focusing
attention upon neighborhood needs to the neglect of the
underlying social forces not necessarily originating in the
neighborhood was pointed out. One leader recommended
that the full energies of those concerned with civic education
should be applied to building up local strength for civic
unity.[3]

Out of a neighborhood philosophy there developed a philosophy of regionalism. The new emphasis lay in the direction
of regional surveys, an extension of boundaries, and in the
planning of large-scale programs adapted to an era of great
mobility and rapid transportation.

3. *Group Organization and Community Organization*

The community movement came to be characterized by the
development of programs of activities in which all the people
in a neighborhood might participate. Such programs were
designed to promote community solidarity, but with the
weakening of neighborhood ties in this period, the appeal of
activities organized on this restricted basis was weakened.
People would participate in group activities of interest to
them, whether within their own neighborhoods or farther
away. In the later stages of the community movement it became necessary to distinguish between group organization
and community organization. According to Jesse Steiner, confusion of these terms prevented proper attention to group
work technique and retarded the adaptation of the community movement to the conditions of the times which required
the development of broad concepts.[4]

[3] White, Eva W., "Local Responsibility for Community Development," *Proceedings of The National Conference of Social Work, 1929*, Chicago: University of Chicago Press, 1929, p. 382.

[4] Steiner, *op. cit.*, p. 339.

The settlements made a significant contribution to group organization by providing individuals and groups with opportunities to participate in self-government, by choosing their own leaders, and by taking on specific responsibilities. When, in 1926, leaders of the settlement movement were asked to project their thinking into the future, Albert J. Kennedy, the historian of the settlement movement, remarked that there was a trend toward distrust of mass activities and a stress upon work with small groups and individuals.[5] Emphasis on the need for clubs, group discussion, and the eliciting of neighborhood leadership gave birth to the techniques that led to the development of the group work method in social work.

Community organization was beginning to utilize the scientific methods being developed for the study of neighborhoods and cities. Surveys and ecological studies like R. D. McKenzie's study of neighborhood life in Columbus, Ohio; community case studies such as those of Walter Pettit and Jesse F. Steiner; and culture analyses such as that of the Lynds' book *Middletown,* published at the end of this period, showed that "disorganization" was the basis for "reorganization." They also showed that there were "natural areas" in cities. Their findings highlighted the salient factors to be worked with, if the community was to be effectively organized.

Community organization started out as a movement closely related to social work and education. Within the field of social work there was a great deal of interest in community organization, but this was not as broad in scope as the community organization movement. Adult education was considered to be very close to it and, according to one authority, should have recognized itself as synonymous with it during World War I.[6]

[5] Kennedy, Albert J., ed., *Settlement Goals for the Next Third of a Century,* Boston: National Federation of Settlements, 1926, preface.

[6] Bowman, Leroy E., "The 1929 Content of the Community Concept," *Journal of Social Forces,* VII, March, 1929, p. 408.

"Community work" was often defined as the aggregate of all efforts to improve social conditions. It was spoken of as preventive work rather than ameliorative, the implication being that social case work picked up the wreckage of the social order, while community work strove to make life healthier and more secure. Its most enthusiastic advocates proposed community organization as a panacea for many social ills.

B. Defense Councils

1. *Origin and Purpose*

The Council of National Defense was organized during World War I. It consisted of the Secretaries of War, Navy, Interior, Agriculture, Commerce, and Labor and a committee of seven civilians. State councils of defense were appointed by the several governors; local community councils were organized with the cooperation of the United States Bureau of Education. The Council of National Defense, in cooperation with the Bureau, sought to mobilize intelligence, food, and money for the war effort through local community organization based on the school. The slogans of the two organizations were: "Every school district a community council for national service," and "Every schoolhouse a community capital and every community a little democracy." [7] As a result, school social centers became centers of community organization. Many states passed legislation permitting the use of schools during after-school hours and provided tax funds for this purpose; the buildings were used by the American Red Cross, YMCA, and other organizations. From this starting point the local defense councils of World War I were developed.

[7] Jackson, Henry E., *The Community Center—What It Is and How to Organize It,* Washington: Government Printing Office, U. S. Bureau of Education, No. 11, 1918, p. 9.

The object of the local community council of national defense was to provide opportunities by which, through continuous teamwork within the neighborhood areas, the people would gradually assume responsibility for the prosecution of the war. They would become accustomed to helping not only in financial campaigns, but also in the work of rehabilitation of soldiers, neighborly home service to the families of men at the front, and work in hospitals. Forums would be provided where they could discuss the issues of the war. In a letter to the chairmen of state councils of defense, President Wilson stated his belief that community councils "will build up from the bottom an understanding and sympathy and unity of purpose and effort which will no doubt have an immediate and decisive effect upon our great undertaking." [8]

In September 1918 community councils of national defense were eight months old and had a nominal membership of one and a quarter million. At this stage they conducted patriotic rallies, made housing surveys, and compiled rooming directories. The Federal Council of National Defense was originally charged with responsibility for research, industrial mobilization, and concentration of material resources for war work, as well as with being a medium through which federal authority reached out to the states and to the general public. Corresponding state councils were similarly designated; county councils also consisted of a small group of appointees. Forty-one states had formally embarked upon community council work.

2. *Form of Organization*

The plan adopted was designed to create a community council which would combine the good features of a federation of agencies and of a community organization in which all citizens held membership. The governing board was to be

[8] Collier, John, "Community Councils—Democracy Every Day I," *Survey*, XL, August, 1918, pp. 605-606.

made up of official representatives of all the social and civic agencies, plus citizens chosen by the people of the community at an open meeting, thus bringing together for maximum performance a group of influential people. The plan was successful, due mainly to the war emergency. The community council work of New York and Chicago will serve to illustrate this phase of the community movement.

New York City was officially requested by the Council of National Defense to promote the organization of defense councils. The Committee on Defense was formed, and authorized an executive committee on Community Councils and Coordination of War Work. This was a Mayor's Committee set up to promote community councils but not to administer them. Through the executive committee the co-operating public and private agencies and the organized citizens were brought together. There was a city advisory committee of agencies, with functional subcommittees. This plan was duplicated throughout the boroughs, districts, and ultimately extended to even the small areas of local community councils of which there were to be over 400. These were groups of individual citizens which were taking on responsibilities as groups and whose members were individually rendering service. The membership of the citizen organizations would break up into groups based on specific tasks undertaken. Delegates, elected by the citizen members of the local community councils, were sent upwards through districts and boroughs to the Greater New York Community Council.

In an attempt to find the ideal area for local council coverage, a compilation was made of the district boundaries of 34 war work and public organizations doing city-wide work on a district basis. When this showed that no two sets of areas coincided, it was decided that community council boundaries would grow by a cleavage process as membership in councils increased.

In the formation of defense councils in New York City, the

announced intention was to organize from the bottom up. It was claimed, however, that as a rule this intention was not carried out, since the governing boards frequently consisted of members appointed from above, and ratification by any more generally representative local body was said to be largely nominal.[9]

Chicago developed "neighborhood committees of defense" consisting of active citizens in each draft-board district. These persons were chosen by the district organizers sent out by the Cook County Auxiliary of the Illinois State Council of Defense. There were 95 draft-board districts in Cook County; of these, 86 were in Chicago. The draft-board district was too large for community council purposes; hence it was broken down into neighborhood committees, which in turn were required to maintain standing committees identical with those of the State Council of Defense. A chairman of the neighborhood committee was elected, and he in turn appointed neighborhood standing committees. These committees elected their own chairmen, who became members of the executive committee of the district organization.

The Chicago plan differed from that of New York City in that it did not seek to develop an organization of agencies to parallel organized citizen groups. Instead it organized the citizenry in a form that closely paralleled the State Council of Defense. John Collier pointed out that this plan did not bring the administrative officials of government and the trained workers of social agencies in touch with one another. It was hoped that "a contagion of technical interest might become possible, until the laity share the enthusiasm of the expert and the expert becomes in a true local sense the adviser and servant of the citizen." [10]

[9] See quotation from "Constitution and By-laws, Community Councils of National Defense in the City of New York," in Daniels, John, *America Via the Neighborhood,* New York: Harper and Bros., 1920, pp. 306-307.

[10] Collier, John, "Community Councils—Democracy Every Day III," *Survey,* XL, September 28, 1918, p. 710.

The twenty-first and twenty-second ward organizations in Chicago were particularly active. These wards corresponded roughly with the Near North Side, where before the war community centers had failed because of the lack of community response. A budget was provided by wealthy women on the Gold Coast—a nearby well-to-do residential district. A paid secretary was engaged and a community service bureau with its own offices was opened. Activities included a house-to-house canvass, mothers' meetings, food demonstrations, community sings, celebrations, and demonstrations. An unusual amount of "neighborliness" grew out of the emotional stress of war.[11]

After the war, when it was thought that community councils might carry into peacetime some of the activity carried on by the defense councils, the twenty-first and twenty-second ward organizations took up the idea, and amid much enthusiasm the Lower North Community Council came into existence. The office of the preceding community service bureau was used as headquarters, and a full-time secretary was retained. Immediately, committees on health, housing, education, industry, forum, and spare time were formed and set to work. Attempts were made to organize blocks after the social unit plan tried in Cincinnati (see below). Sanitary conditions were investigated and recreation activities were organized. The office became a center for information and advice. However, after the enthusiasm of organization had passed and the activities of the Council settled into a routine, the volunteers drifted into other activities. The Council ran into debt. The "social block" experiments went to pieces. By 1921 the affairs of the Lower North Community Council had reached a crisis and a meeting was called to determine whether it would not be better to discontinue the Council. A few retained interest in it. The secretary resigned, the

[11] Zorbaugh, Harvey W., *The Gold Coast and the Slum,* Chicago: University of Chicago Press, 1929, p. 204.

budget was cut in half, and for a while the Council drifted along as best it could in the face of apathy and with no well-defined policy. Whatever the contributions of the defense councils to peacetime neighborhood organization they were not to be made by a mere imitation or extension of wartime efforts.

C. School Centers

1. *Growth of School Centers*

A survey of school centers, conducted in 1919, failed to indicate an increase in the wider use of schools after the war. There were 667 centers in 107 cities. A "center" was defined as "a school which is used regularly at least one evening a week for two or more activities—or twice a week for one— not counting night schools." [12] There was an apparent decrease in the number of school centers throughout the period 1916 to 1923.

Eleanor T. Glueck suggested some possible explanations. These can be summarized:

1) Differences in the definitions used—those of 1919 and 1923 were less inclusive than that of 1916.
2) Lack of response to questionnaires sent out by private organizations—the 1916 questionnaire had been distributed by the United States Bureau of Education.
3) It may also be that the numerous community buildings and church social centers which have flourished since the war lessened the demand for the community center in the school building.
4) It may be that although schools are widely used their use does not meet the requirements of the definition. [13]

[12] Perry, Clarence A., *School Center Gazette, 1919-1920,* New York: Russell Sage Foundation, 1920, p. 3.
[13] Glueck, Eleanor T., *Community Use of Schools,* Baltimore: Williams and Wilkins, 1927, pp. 35-36.

A report on school centers for 1920 showed that about half were supported entirely by taxation; the financial burden for the other half was either shared by people using the facilities or raised by voluntary subscriptions.[14]

In Chicago in 1924 there were 15 community centers which received an appropriation of from three to eight hundred dollars per year from tax funds.[15] One group of interested people urged that 15 more should be organized. They recommended that a director of community centers should be appointed in the office of the superintendent of schools and suggested that a budget of $80,000 be paid out of school funds for the promotion of such activities.

In New York the Board of Education operated between 200 and 300 community centers in the schools, in addition to which a considerable number were maintained by private organizations. In 1924 the neighborhood organizations that had been meeting in the public schools of Brooklyn since about 1913 formed the "Brooklyn Federation of Community Centers."

2. Aids in Community Organization

A local community center association consisting of all the different groups that made their headquarters in the school building was looked upon as doing "community organization." Foremost in the activities of the "social" or "community" centers was recreation. There were also adult education activities such as neighborhood forums and such "community services" as libraries, health work, and vocational bureaus.

Some educators regarded community organization as a tool for adult education. At the meeting of the National Uni-

[14] *The Community Center,* New York: National Community Center Association, October–December, 1920, p. 90.
[15] Gillin, J. L., "Economic Aspects of the Community that Determine the Nature and Extent of Comprehensive Democratic Organization," *Proceedings of the National Conference of Social Work,* 1925, pp. 354-359.

versity Extension Association in 1919, Edward L. Burchard cited a public health exhibition at a Chicago high school as an example. A community council had been formed, consisting of representatives from music, labor, and businessmen's organizations. This council had then set up a series of educational groups. The children of the school had helped with the exhibits. Burchard commented:

You have first the children being used to react educationally on the neighborhood. Then you have the neighborhood coming in through its different groups, and legislation on the outside on such questions as how to clean up their immediate neighborhood, how to reduce tuberculosis, and how to improve in various other ways. Now I call that an ultimate educational extension unit that cannot be beaten.[16]

Some believed that community organization in the neighborhood offered the best opportunity for finding unity underneath religious and cultural differences, and a method which would revolutionize politics. Mary Follett proposed that people should organize themselves into neighborhood groups to express their needs, desires, and aspirations. These needs should become the substance of politics, she contended, and the neighborhood groups should become recognized political units. Through neighborhood organization Miss Follett hoped that men would learn that they were not to *influence* politics but to *be* politics. She regarded the community center movement as the most deliberate and conscious movement for neighborhood organization.[17]

3. *School Centers Fell Short*

The school center fell short of Ward's goal that it become "the Citizens' Council Chamber" for the discovery of com-

[16] In Perry, Clarence A., "School Center History in Chicago," *Journal of Social Forces*, III, January, 1925, p. 293. Quoted from the *Proceedings of the National University Extension Association*, Chicago, January, 1919.

[17] Follett, Mary, *The New State*, New York: Longmans, Green and Company, 1918, pp. 203-242.

mon interests and greater control of legislation by the people, and it did not approach the ideals set for it by the leaders of the community organization movement. It did not become the ideal community organization in which the people of a community could become concerned about their common needs and assume active responsibility for their common affairs. The school centers were not fulfilling these ideals. They were neither self-supporting nor self-governing; few school centers functioned throughout the year, and with their increasing emphasis upon recreational activities, they neglected the civic, economic, and cultural phases of community betterment.

During this period the old neighborhood structure of many large cities was breaking down; recent immigrants moving into a locale did not feel at home in the unfamiliar centers and, generally speaking, evinced no great interest in them. In the community centers of the near North Side (referred to above) which were part of the Chicago school center movement before World War I, there was little response from the community. Children came to the playgrounds, and a few mothers came to the movies, but the men were conspicuously absent. It was not enough merely to open the doors and expect people to come together to discuss politics or local affairs. As a result of the lack of attendance the doors were closed.[18]

There was a growing recognition that before people could act intelligently on problems of mutual concern they must first attain a group consciousness and an understanding of these problems. The many barriers of race, religion, differences in education and in social and economic status which existed among the people of many neighborhoods would have to be overcome in the process of organizing the community.

[18] Zorbaugh, *op. cit.*, p. 203.

D. Social Unit Experiment

1. *Purpose and Origin*

The purpose of the Cincinnati Social Unit Experiment was to promote a type of democratic community organization through which the citizenship as a whole could participate directly in the control of community affairs, while at the same time making constant use of the highest technical skill available. The experiment sought to make social work democratic and to do away with the benevolent paternalism characteristic of many agencies. It was one of a number of experiments in community organization current at this time, in which the dominant fundamental philosophy was that of democratic participation.

The social unit idea had its beginnings in the experimental work of Mr. and Mrs. Wilbur C. Phillips, executives of the Milwaukee Child Welfare Commission, who carried on a health center experiment during the period 1911-1912. After leaving Milwaukee, Mr. and Mrs. Phillips prepared a manuscript based on their Milwaukee experience outlining the social unit plan. Some social workers and medical people became interested in the new plan and held a meeting in Washington in 1915 to consider the possibility of putting it into effect. The following year there was established in New York the National Social Unit Organization with Gifford Pinchot as its first president and Mr. and Mrs. Phillips as its first secretaries. A fund of $90,000 was raised to finance a demonstration for three years.

2. *Principles and Organization*

The plan was based upon the three following principles: (1) Citizens of the community are to be organized into small primary units so that they will know the problems, conditions and people of the area and so that the elected representative of such a primary unit will know all these aspects of the situation as a neighbor. This "geographic citizenship representative" should also be a worker in the community organization in order to have the "training of service." (2) Those who, because of special knowledge or skill, are serving the community in a direct or advisory capacity should be organized with reference to units of population served, so that they will be in close touch with the citizens and their representatives. The theory was that each citizen should be represented both geographically and occupationally. (3) There should be "an organic and co-ordinate working relationship" between the representatives of the occupational and geographical groupings.[19]

A district of about 15,000 people was desired to test the soundness of this method. Cincinnati was already planning an intensive experiment in district health work and pledged $45,000 toward the cost of operation of the social unit experiment. With $90,000 raised by the national organization, the total budget available was $135,000 for the three years.

Although the social unit experiment was fostered and financed largely by the national organization, a vigorous campaign was waged for Cincinnati to get the demonstration. The plan was presented in detail through a series of meetings held by the leading social, health, and civic organizations and attended by some 500 to 600 people. Thus, prior to the initiation of the experiment, there were a number of influential leaders ready to support it. The first organization meeting was attended by more than 600 persons, representative of almost every trade and profession, as well as of a number of other groups. At this meeting the Cincinnati Social Unit Organization was formed, with the mayor as honorary executive. A purely advisory city-wide organization was built up,

[19] Dinwiddie, Courtenay, *Community Responsibility* (A Review of the Cincinnati Social Unit Experiment), New York: New York School of Social Work, 1922, pp. 1-2.

inclusive of citizen and occupational councils nominated by the various neighborhoods and groups in the city.

There was considerable competition among the districts in the city interested in being selected for the experiment. After three months' deliberation the Mohawk-Brighton District was chosen. It had demonstrated its interest by organizing a campaign committee under whose auspices public meetings were held, endorsements of local organizations were secured, and petitions were signed by a large number of residents. The final choice of district was made at a public meeting attended by 500 people, many of whom were Mohawk-Brighton residents, who set forth the advantages of the experiment to their community.

The experiment got under way in the summer of 1917. The committee of over 200 Mohawk-Brighton residents which had so actively campaigned to secure the unit began to organize, and on September 27, 1917, a representative district organization was formed.

The Mohawk-Brighton Social Unit Organization was made up of: (1) A "Citizens' Council," consisting of 31 block representatives (or "block workers"), each chosen by a Block Council which was in turn elected by all those over 18 years of age living in a given block; (2) an "Occupational Council," made up of the elected representatives of the occupational groups (physicians, nurses, social workers, clergymen, teachers, businessmen, Central Labor Council of the city, and later of the recreational workers of the district); and (3) a "General Council," which was the governing body, consisting of the citizens' and occupational councils together.

3. Results of Experiment

From one point of view the social unit was an intensive demonstration in the field of public health. However, the fundamental purpose of the demonstration was to test the value of a new type of organization; the health activities were simply a means to this end. Among the most novel features of this form of organization was the mingling of policy-making and executive functions in the Citizens' Council which was part of the theory of the plan. Another distinguishing feature was representation by occupational groups.

The claims made for the democratic nature of the experiment were challenged, both as to methods and purposes. It was suggested that its plan of organization might easily lay it open to the charge of clever manipulation and arbitrary control by outside leadership, even though there was close integration of occupational and neighborhood groups by which the social unit retained control of its own affairs. The Chairman of the Council of Social Agencies stated that it was not a "natural" experiment in which the need for community organization was discovered first and the social unit followed. With a large fund of money and capable executives, it was said that the plan would appeal to almost any community and the community would go through the procedure of being grateful, regardless of how well it understood the plan.

The very nature of the experiment made it necessary for its promoters to be chosen as its executives. Their preconceived ideas on program may very well have influenced the decisions of the general council. These factors, which may have been operative in the initiation of the plan, were not inherent in the plan itself. Its controls were devised so that they would not fall into the hands of a small group. Despite the contention that the executives had the machinery for getting acceptance of any program they proposed, Edward T. Devine could find no trace of machine politics in his study of the situation.[20]

Because of the tenseness due to the war situation there was a good deal of fear of anything that might be critical of the

[20] Devine, Edward T., "The Social Unit in Cincinnati," *Survey*, November, 1919, pp. 115-126.

existing government. Consequently, when the Mayor of Cincinnati charged that the social unit was being promoted for antigovernmental and socialistic purposes, public support was alienated and the progress of the work was hampered. Besides, the general excitement over the influenza epidemic of 1918 and the opposition to the experiment of certain politicians at City Hall had a deterring effect on the successful operation of the plan. In spite of these obstacles most of the projected organization was set up and functioned for the three year period proposed. The experiment was discontinued in 1920, when outside support was withdrawn.

In summing up the results of the Cincinnati Social Unit Experiment Devine stated that it brought about more thorough and constructive diagnosis of the needs of families in trouble and prompted neighborliness and sociability. Stuart Queen saw in the neighborhood work a decrease in "uplift" and an increase in neighborhood organization for self-expression. He observed that there was less philanthropy and more working together of whole neighborhoods in the development of service by democratically organized professional groups.[21]

Writing in 1920, John Daniels referred to attempts being made to relate the National Social Unit Organization to the community councils of New York City. He hastened to add in a footnote, however, that the "New York partnership of councils and unit" was discontinued.[22]

E. Community Councils

1. *In Neighborhoods and Districts*

With the development of the community organization movement there arose the concept of the community council which brought together representatives of various agencies

---

[21] Queen, *op. cit.*, pp. 141-143.
[22] Daniels, John, *America Via the Neighborhood*, New York: Harper and Bros., 1920, pp. 311-312.

and organizations concerned with social welfare. Community councils were organized not only on a city-wide basis but also in neighborhoods and districts. The need for separate auspices for sponsoring services and for interagency coordination was becoming clearer.

There was much discussion in this period around definitions of "community." The organizational form and the activities of community councils depended to a large extent upon the definition of community that was accepted. Past efforts in local neighborhood organization, varying in purpose and method, left an accumulation of many different forms of organization. Many of the local councils of national defense had survived and were adapting themselves to local purposes.

In accordance with differing definitions of community and neighborhood, various forms of organization were advocated. "Local community" as defined by Clarence A. Perry meant the "local acquaintance range" of the ordinary citizen.[23] It is a residential area in which propinquity relationships have not been wholly superseded by special interest associations. Those people who lived within easy walking distance of one another were considered to be in the same neighborhood. It was believed that the social function which suffered most from the atrophy of neighborhood communities was that of fellowship (companionship, friendship, sociability, comradeship, or courtship). It was suggested that social workers concentrate on the provision of the means for what were called "fellowship functions." [24]

Definitions of community were based on organizational as well as geographic factors, as implied in earlier discussions of the community organization movement. The term "community," said David Snedden, denotes "any social organization

[23] Perry, Clarence Arthur, "The Rehabilitation of the Local Community," *Journal of Social Forces*, IV, March, 1926, p. 558.
[24] Snedden, David, "Neighborhoods and Neighborliness," *Journal of Social Forces*, V, December, 1926, p. 236.

occupying a defined geographic area and embracing all the inhabitants of that area," such as a county, village, city, or nation.[25] According to J. H. Montgomery, "community" is a group of leaders of the various social and civic organizations in a given locality. This definition is reminiscent of the earlier discussion of councils of social agencies. The definition includes not only social work organizations but educational, civic, moral, and even economic organizations. A community council would be a clearinghouse through which the leaders of all these organizations would know what the other organizations were doing. Duplication of effort could be prevented, and neglected areas could be discovered. Montgomery proposed that the larger city or county council should take the initiative in developing local community councils.[26]

The tendency to jump from the strictly local or neighborhood unit to the city as a whole was deplored by Albert J. Kennedy. He urged the use of the district as a unit because of its greater degree of stability and obvious natural boundaries, such as existed in the case of a former town incorporated within a large city. Kennedy suggested district coordinating councils on specific aspects of district life—for example, a district health council. Although "health" was the magic word at the time, he maintained that employment, recreation, and education would each in turn have its day. The district council would be made up of delegates from organizations in any way involved in the particular district problem under consideration.[27]

An interesting example of functional coordination at the district level was the East Harlem Health Center in New York City. It was conducted in the period immediately fol-

[25] *Ibid.*, p. 231.

[26] Montgomery, J. H., "Principles of Organization in Community Councils," *Journal of Social Forces*, V, September, 1926, pp. 95-97.

[27] Kennedy, Albert J., "The District as a Unit for Community Organization," *Journal of Social Forces*, V, March, 1927, pp. 458-461.

lowing World War I when the American Red Cross took on public health as a major peacetime activity. The New York Chapter requested and received funds from the national organization for a three year demonstration of a health center in East Harlem with the following purpose:

To demonstrate the methods and the value of the coordination of all health and kindred activities in a defined local area, including about 100,000 people; to demonstrate the methods and the value of a well-rounded health program in any one district of the city, such programs to be secured through the coordination of agencies already existing and working in the district, and the establishment of such additional agencies as are needed to make a fairly complete health program for the district.[28]

A director was appointed and in January, 1921, 22 agencies joined formally in the project. There were two nursing, four family welfare, eleven health agencies, and five "community agencies," such as settlements. The agencies devoted to nursing, family welfare, and health used the center for their health activities but continued to use their own locations for other services. Wherever possible, one of the existing agencies was asked to extend its services to fill in the gaps in service.

The Center was managed by a Council, an Executive Committee, and an Executive Officer. The Council consisted of 15 representatives from the cooperating agencies, 15 representatives from the district, and 15 members from the Executive and Health Service Committees of the Red Cross. It had no authority over the activities of the cooperating agencies, but it was concerned with the operation of the building, the establishment of health activities not already carried on in the Center, and the promotion of the general aims of the demonstration. An Executive Committee of 11 members was

[28] Bowman, Leroy E., "Tangible Results of Coordination of Health and Family Welfare Work in a Defined City Area," *Journal of Social Forces*, IV, December, 1925, pp. 340-341.

elected by the Council to carry on its business between meetings. An Executive Officer, appointed by the Chairman of
the Red Cross County Chapter subject to the approval of
the Council, acted as the representative of the Red Cross and
served as a liaison officer among the agencies. He was directly
responsible to the Executive Committee of the Council.[29]

In the beginning no two of the participating organizations
covered the same areas. Inasmuch as the Public Health Department was the agency offering the largest number of services, its district boundaries were used to define the Center's
area of service. Working arrangements were made with the
family agencies, since they were the only ones that did not
redistrict. Within two years all of the clinics originated by
the Red Cross had sufficiently proved their place in the
district health program to be taken over by local agencies
operating in those fields.

The work of the Center was believed to have had a notice-
ably good effect on the health of the district. The decrease
in mortality was said to have been quite definitely accelerated.[30] The Director of the Center believed that it had stimulated interest in health problems on the part of the settlement
leaders, school principals, and businessmen of the community. A better relationship had developed between the community and a number of city-wide agencies, and it was
believed that the foundation had been laid for a comprehensive neighborhood association, in which local residents would
have more initiative and control and in which the Health
Center would participate as a constituent member.[31]

In addition to this type of functional coordination which
was set up on a district basis, there existed in New York
City, during this period and for some time previous, five
major types of community organization at the neighborhood

[29] *Ibid.*, p. 342.
[30] *Ibid.*, p. 344.
[31] *Ibid.*, p. 345.

level: settlements, neighborhood associations, community centers operated by the Board of Education, independent community center associations meeting in the schools, and the community councils. After a year of conferences by delegates from each of the central federations, the Community Committee of New York City was formed in 1923. As a common service body through which acquaintance and understanding of the various organizations was to be fostered, the Committee prepared exhibits, studies of population, health, recreation, and employment, and built up systematic knowledge of several hundred community groups.

2. *At the City-wide Level*

One of the theories of community organization current in this period considered the community to be "organized" when its most important agencies formed a federation or council through which they worked together to improve social conditions and the quality and quantity of social service available to the community. The national social service agencies, on the other hand, regarded community organization as the establishment of a local unit of their own organization. The community organization movement made its furthest advance, however, through the coordination of social agencies in the local community. With the development of this movement, as sketched below, it became evident that neighborhood and district forms of organization had a significant role.

When the problem of a large number of unrelated private social agencies arose, the charity organization society assumed responsibility as a "community organization" to coordinate these efforts and to give leadership in movements to improve social conditions.[32] The first central council of social agencies came into being when the Pittsburgh Associated Charities,

[32] Watson, Frank D., *The Charity Organization Movement in the United States*, New York: Macmillan, 1922, pp. 422-423.

seeking to emphasize its clearinghouse functions, became more of an association of charities than a society for "organizing charity." When its constitution was revised it became a member agency of the Central Council of Social Agencies which it originally sponsored. The war gave a great impetus to this movement. Up until the war only six major cities had councils in operation; within a few years after the war, councils of social agencies were established in many of the larger cities, as well as many others of variant types that had sprung into existence in smaller cities. In practically all instances the movement for some such coordinating body had its origin in the charity organization movement.

Councils of social agencies were set up to develop higher standards of work, to eliminate duplication of effort, and to meet needs not adequately met. It was a device for bringing together the various specialized agencies so that they could act jointly. It had only advisory powers, and its administrative sphere was limited to its own internal affairs. It would meet regularly to review the general situation in the field of social work, to plan improvements in services and more effective cooperation among agencies, and to decide which agency was best suited to fulfill particular functions. Although the central council was often largely the result of efforts of the charity organization society, it functioned most effectively when separated from the internal affairs of the charity organization society. Francis McLean characterized it as "essentially a body composed of official delegates from social agencies." [33] This did not preclude members-at-large, for which all councils provided. In fact, it might be necessary where the agencies were "unprogressive" for one-third of the total to consist of members-at-large. The presence of a central council would not render superfluous the work of a civic

[33] McLean, Francis, *The Central Council of Social Agencies*, New York: American Association for Organizing Family Social Work, 1920, p. 5.

organization interested in social conditions; there would be points of contact with the central council, and there would have to be constant exchange and understanding between these organizations and the central council. McLean advocated that, in the properly organized central council, the consensus of opinion of the paid and volunteer workers in the agencies should be reflected. These people were in day-to-day contact with concrete social problems, and because of their practical experience they were in a position to make valid contributions to the council's work.

Other methods of community organization, such as financial federations, also came into being at this time.[34] These provided for joint collection of funds for the private social agencies of a community. It was argued that a financial federation provided for more efficient collection, less annoyance to those solicited, more givers, larger contributions, social education, and greater cooperation in social work. As a result of a study of financial federations in 1917, a special committee of the American Association for Organizing Charity recommended against the adoption of the plan of financial federation at that time because of insufficient evidence of its effectiveness and apprehension lest federations be developed that would not be "socially" organized, that is, shaped by leading social workers and businessmen already active in social work.[35] The war and war chests accelerated the growth of financial federations. From 1922 to 1928 the number increased from 49 to 297 and the amount raised from $23,656,000 to $63,397,000. The movement toward coordination of social agencies continued through 1929, as did the conflict between those who emphasized joint financing as the central idea and those who opposed it.

[34] Watson, *op. cit.*, pp. 120-121. For early history of financial federations, see pp. 419 ff.

[35] *Report of the Special Committee on Financial Federations*, American Association for Organizing Charity, 1917, p. 65.

One of the first comprehensive outlines of the organization of an over-all welfare planning council incorporating provision for planning by neighborhoods as well as by functional fields, was presented in 1925 in the plan of organization of the Welfare Council of New York City. On the objective which should be adopted for the Welfare Council, one social worker was quoted as saying: "We are going to educate the coming generation in the needs for, and methods of the various social agencies so that in the future, instead of depending upon a few socially-minded wealthy people to support our agencies, we shall have a community-wide understanding and interest in their work which should go far toward securing the necessary basic reforms to prevent the ills we now seek to cure, as well as assuring continued support to social work." [36] The Council was to seek impetus from the interest of both the administrators of social work and those who supported it with money, intelligence, and good will.

"Regional organization," including the setting up of borough conferences, was suggested as a later stage of development for the Welfare Council. District conferences could be set up within boroughs. Such conferences, it was thought, might result in common housing for the agencies in the district, or demonstration projects under joint auspices. The Welfare Council would make provision for relating such district organization to its divisions.

There were at least eight organizations in New York City known as neighborhood associations whose purpose was to bring individuals together, to encourage cooperation among agencies, to aid in governmental activities, and to act as a community clearinghouse for the district. These neighborhood associations had purposes within their respective districts which crossed the lines of the over-all council divisions.

[36] Persons, W. Frank, *The Welfare Council of New York City*, New York: The Welfare Council of New York City, 1925, p. 64.

Because they were community and not functional organizations it was proposed that they should constitute a section of the Recreation, Education, and Neighborhood Division. Correlation of their activities would be more difficult to work out than that between a division and a functional service, as in the case of the East Harlem Health Center described in the preceding section. It was proposed that the neighborhood associations have freedom for direct civic action and that they be self-supporting and strictly independent in matters of civic or community policy. Serious consideration was given to a suggestion that the Welfare Council should formulate a city-wide plan for neighborhood conferences of social agencies. The eight existing neighborhood associations were to form the nucleus of the Council's committee on neighborhood organization and community districting. In relation to the Welfare Council these conferences would be advisory in character. Their purpose would be to stimulate greater unity in local work and to develop neighborhood understanding, support, and cooperation with the local civic bodies by utilizing neighborhood loyalty. It was suggested that an assistant secretary of the Welfare Council be made available to the coordinated neighborhood associations in order to maintain mutually helpful relations between them and the central service bureaus and the divisions. In this way the coordinated neighborhood associations would, in effect, be affiliated with the Welfare Council. At the same time they would be able to carry on their own civic activities independently of the policies and activities of the Welfare Council.

Looking at this period in broad perspective we can see how the concept of community and the development of the community organization movement influenced neighborhood organization. The social welfare problem shifted from the prevention of pauperism to the organization of the community. The social institutions that were designed to work on this problem found that the interorganizational council at city, district, and neighborhood levels helped them reach the people they sought to serve. In the next period we shall see the rapid spread of such councils.

CHAPTER IV

THE SPREAD OF COMMUNITY COUNCILS

A. Background: 1929 to World War II

1. *The Great Depression*

The great depression struck in 1929. In the spring there were already 2,860,000 unemployed. By January, 1930, the number had risen to over four million; by the end of 1930, it had reached nearly seven million; the increase continued steadily, to a peak of 13 to 15 million unemployed in the spring of 1933.[1]

Attention was sharply focused on the local community, because responsibility for relief was local. Many novel forms of voluntary neighborhood help were worked out, such as the "block-aid" scheme described in a later section of this chapter. In some communities, neighborhood or community councils were organized as a means whereby the social agencies and local residents could meet to discuss the relief situation.

Many governmental and industrial leaders regarded pov-

---

[1] Brown, Josephine C., *Public Relief: 1929-1939,* New York: Henry Holt and Co., 1940, pp. 64-65.

erty as the result of personal abnormality or incompetence and were opposed to emergency public measures for relief. They argued that poverty is the concern of those who desire to be charitable rather than the responsibility of the entire community. According to this point of view, private charity was an essential method of dealing with problems of family dependency. Such a philosophy of economic individualism regarded increased public responsibility for relief as both unfortunate and wrong. However, the necessity for increased governmental provision resulted in the opening up of new relief categories and showed that the philosophy of voluntary provision was not in accord with the direction of events.

When the Works Progress Administration was being set up to provide useful employment at a "security wage" to some of the unemployed, it was found that by December 1, 1935, there were 4,885,000 persons certified as employable under WPA. These persons represented the breadwinners of 3,250,000 families.[2]

With the passage of the Social Security Act in 1935 it was recognized that unemployment was one of the vicissitudes of the economy and that since the country as a whole was affected, the federal government must assume responsibility for insuring the large numbers of unemployed persons exposed to these risks. The conviction was growing that the individual had a right to society's help.

2. *Effect on Family Life*

Even before the financial crash of 1929 the National Federation of Settlements, with the cooperation of over 100 settlements, gathered case studies through which neighbors told their own stories of life in the industrial districts of American cities. The experience of neighborhoods in 32

[2] Colcord, Joanna C., "Relief, Style 1936," *Proceedings of the National Conference of Social Work, 1936*, Chicago: University of Chicago Press, 1936, p. 291.

cities and 21 states was drawn upon: the tenements of New York, the textile districts of Philadelphia, the auto center at Detroit, the stockyards of Chicago, and the valleys of the Pittsburgh steel district.

These studies showed that "broken work" was not only a symptom of a financial crisis but a recurrent fault of modern production.[3] A youth of 19 in one of the families in which there was unemployment put it this way:

Unemployment. The curse of modern civilization. It demoralizes the family, weakens the body and mind, destroys our faith in human beings, brings about chaos and controversies and worriment and arguments and quarrels and fights within the family, causes impoverished conditions in the home, and makes discontented, dejected and disheartened people. . . . It is only with the severest economy that we are able to exist comfortably without luxury. But when any member is without work we can not meet expenses. We are compelled by necessity to resort to evil, shady, or underhand methods to secure necessities. . . . We become corrupt during the long interval of unemployment. . . .[4]

Out of these conditions of unemployment and family breakdown it was not surprising that juvenile delinquency became an urgent social problem. One of the significant developments in neighborhood organization in this period was the number and variety of projects to combat juvenile delinquency on a neighborhood basis. The fact was stressed that the many agencies serving youth must coordinate their efforts in a concerted plan so that these services would be available to those who needed them. In some projects the council of social agencies was felt to be the most effective coordinator at the neighborhood level. In many instances an approach was used similar to that which in the previous

[3] Elderton, Marion, ed., *Case Studies of Unemployment*, Philadelphia: University of Pennsylvania Press, 1931, pp. xiii-xv. Compiled by the Unemployment Committee of the National Federation of Settlements.
[4] *Ibid.*, p. 385.

period had brought health centers into being. A program of direct service was organized as part of an "area project" to prevent juvenile delinquency.

3. *Community Councils*

Writing in 1930, Leroy Bowman observed that community organizers were less doctrinaire as to the ideal form of civic or social integration than they had been previously. He referred to the "community religion" of a few years before when people were being recruited into community organizations "democratic in the extreme and supposedly dominated by neighborly sentiments." [5]

Whether the initial impetus had come from the need for unemployment relief, recreation, education, or from concern about juvenile delinquency, there was a tendency among community councils to broaden their interests to include the general welfare of the community. Some councils of social agencies recognized this and made efforts to tie in neighborhood organization with coordination and planning for the larger community.

B. Neighborhoods in Distress

1. *Block-Aid*

Among the many types of voluntary neighborhood schemes for relieving the suffering caused by unemployment at the beginning of the depression, the block-aid plan in New York City is an interesting example of a direct-service project organized on a block basis. It was derived from the Man-a-Block Plan which originated in Buffalo, where the residents of a city block pooled their chores into a full-time job on a paid basis for some unemployed man. Block-aid in New York City was a door-to-door, block-by-block collection of small

[5] Bowman, Leroy E., "Community Organization," *American Journal of Sociology,* XXXV, May, 1930, p. 1008.

sums by which it was hoped to continue financing the program of the New York City Emergency Work Bureau through the summer of 1932. The anticipated goal was two million dollars. The campaign was backed by prominent men and women and was directed by the John Price Jones Corporation, which used its own supervisors but employed about 1,500 unemployed white collar workers for the mass of clerical work. This made it a work project in its own right. Another by-product claimed for the scheme by its sponsors was to be the strengthening of neighborliness and the widening of community understanding and responsibility.[6]

Branch organizations with distinguished chairmen were set up in each of the five boroughs, which in turn were divided into districts, 165 in all, with some 30 to 190 blocks in a district. Each district was staffed with a secretary, auditor, and clerical force behind which stood a local committee of prominent citizens. District chairmen assumed responsibility for securing a chairman and treasurer for each block in their territory, and the block chairmen agreed to secure volunteer service from ten or more "block-aiders," that is, solicitors. Each block-aider promised to secure ten or more contributors.

The object of block-aid was to provide a subsistence wage of $15 per week for a man for 20 weeks. When a block had $300 assured a man was put to work. The block-aider had authentic case stories to illustrate the need. Subscriptions extended over a period of 20 weeks and could be collected weekly by the block-aider. The plan was quite limited since the anticipated goal of two million dollars would keep only a small fraction of New York's unemployed men at work for the 20 week period.

Another example of neighborhood organization arising from the relief crisis was the development of community

---

[6] Springer, Gertrude, "Block-Aid," *The Survey*, LXVIII, May, 1932, pp. 182-183.

councils in Pittsburgh, described in the last section of this chapter.

2. *For the Public Welfare*

Early in 1936 the Department of Social Security of the State of Washington instructed local administrators in all 39 counties of the state to become active in the development and stimulation of local community councils. This was done because it was feared by the department that the new social security program was going to encourage an attitude of "leave it to the state" and thus promote a tendency for "local resources of money, interest, and helpfulness to dry up." [7]

The councils were started, or encouraged to start, in order to promote coordination and central planning by a representative delegate body. The department wanted to supplement its own efforts with the informal resources of the community and the volunteer activity of individuals and groups. It was felt that community councils would create an awareness of social problems and needs and of the help the community could offer toward assimilating the new public welfare program in a natural way—by rooting it "in the soil of the accustomed." [8]

Through its community organization section the Department of Social Security of the State of Washington attempted to stimulate and guide the development of local community councils through its local administrators. Some field visits were made by state staff, usually at the request of the local community. The department thought of its role as only temporary. The State Conference of Social Work was suggested as a sponsoring body if it could find the resources.

This development was of some importance because it in-

[7] Hall, John, "The Administration and Supervision of Community Councils," *Yearbook of the National Probation Association, 1937*, New York: National Probation Assoc., 1937, p. 29.

[8] *Ibid.*, p. 30.

volved a public welfare department initiating and stimulating the development of community councils to coordinate public and voluntary efforts in the social services, and furthermore, it was a state department stimulating such developments in localities throughout the state.

C. Settlements and School Centers

1. *Changing Perspectives*

The settlement faced many difficulties in this period. Old neighborhoods disappeared and new neighbors were not always sympathetic to the aims of the settlement. Also, the settlement found itself in the midst of a "new poor" who knew the material advantages life could offer but were thwarted in attaining them.[9] Settlements met changed conditions by shifting the emphasis of their work, by adopting and helping the new neighbors, or by moving to other neighborhoods.

The settlements were committed to modifications of program and were developing new methods of work. Through the "club" the settlement staff had an opportunity to make the acquaintance of individuals and groups under conditions of freedom and to discover what natural and instinctive powers, capacities, and desires individuals and groups had. The most important settlement activity was considered to be "promoting free association between individuals and groups."[10]

Helen Hart proposed for the settlement "the objective of personality development through group relations."[11] To carry through the proposed objective, the settlement held

[9] Hart, Helen, "Changing Function of the Settlement," *Proceedings of the National Conference of Social Work, 1931*, Chicago: University of Chicago Press, 1931, p. 291.

[10] Kennedy, Albert J., "Social Settlements," *Social Work Year Book, 1929*, New York: Russell Sage Foundation, 1929, p. 424.

[11] *Op. cit.*, p. 292.

an advantage over the public school because it enlisted far
more of the child's emotional interest through the life situations which the child experienced in informal groups. But
it was not enough merely to include this emphasis in the
large assortment of activities already carried by the settlement. Miss Hart recommended that settlements make a major
adjustment in their programs and emphasize group work
skills throughout.

School centers were also meeting with difficulties. As noted
above, the earlier hope that the community center and the
school would come together was not being realized. This was
due in part to the opposition by some groups to extending
the educational system and in part to the opposition of the
political parties who felt threatened by the civic activity in
the community center. The attractiveness of the school community center decreased in view of the increased attractiveness of commercial forms of leisure-time activity. The New
York City Board of Education which had offered free public
lectures in its school halls as far back as 1890 discontinued
these programs in 1929. They had lost popularity with the
advent of the motion picture and the radio. The activities
in the public schools, excluding formal classes, became chiefly
recreational.[12]

2. *A Joint Project*

In Cleveland an interesting experiment was conducted
jointly by a social settlement and the Community Center
Department of the public schools in the Anthony Wayne
neighborhood.[13] Although it was inaugurated in 1925 it continued for several years. It is presented here, not as a development typical of the period, but rather as a conscious effort to

[12] Perry, Clarence A. and Williams, Marguerita P., *New York School Centers and Their Community Policy*, New York: Russell Sage Foundation, 1931,
p. 7.

[13] North, Cecil C., *The Community and Social Welfare*, New York: McGraw
Hill, 1931, pp. 268-269.

amalgamate the experience of the settlement and the school center.

Hiram House Social Settlement wanted to take its program more directly to the people and to try a new approach. It selected a neighborhood in which there was no social settlement. The Community Center Department of the public schools was willing to combine its community center activities with the program of the settlement.

An elementary school was selected in a neighborhood where there were a number of people who had at one time or another attended Hiram House. One of the reasons for its selection was that a school concerned with younger children offered greater possibilities of establishing contacts with the home and stimulating cooperation between home and school. This was considered more important than the more adequate facilities of a larger school. Because of lack of space Hiram House maintained a neighborhood office nearby for which the Board of Education shared the cost of heat, light, equipment, and one-fifth of the annual budget. A member of the settlement staff became director of the combined neighborhood and school center program, his salary being a joint responsibility of both groups. He and his family took up residence in the neighborhood. His staff, made up of several full-time workers and a number of part-time students in training, was financed by the settlement and the center. The director attended staff meetings of the Department of Community Centers, cooperated in all city-wide programs pertaining to centers, and was free to develop additional plans or meet local needs as the situation indicated.[14]

The program attempted to deal with the family and neighborhood as a unit, seeking the cooperation of parents, day school, church, and other neighborhood groups through in-

[14] Graham, Perle D., "The Cleveland Study of Community Centers from the Standpoint of the Schools and Private Effort," *Proceedings of the National Conference of Social Work, 1931,* Chicago: University of Chicago Press, 1931, pp. 324-325.

timate person-to-person contacts. The program in the school building was the usual school center program of recreational activities for adults and young people 15 years of age and over. There was, in addition, an extensive program of club and small group meetings carried out into the streets, vacant lots, and homes of the neighborhood. A leader gathered an informal group anywhere by offering to help them play; he returned to the same place the following week and gradually established a regularity of meeting. Eventually, such a "club" might be invited to use one of the homes as a regular meeting place. Contact with parents was established in this way, and opportunities were presented for helping parents to a better understanding of some of the health and behavior problems of their children. In addition to working with the family— which was considered a fundamental part of the whole group work program—the club leader also acted as a liaison between the home and the school when problems of adjustment arose. Parents as a rule readily accepted the leader as the "club teacher" from the school.

One of the objectives of the program was to build better recreational, educational, and cultural activities around the home and school in order to preserve normal family and neighborhood life. The program included helping individuals with personal problems; facilitating the work of the school to function in the home, and thus raise the standard of civic ideals and civic pride; extending the services of the school, the settlement, and other agencies deeper into the life of the neighborhood; demonstrating that this work should and could be taken over by the schools eventually.

In this instance of settlement and school center cooperation we see them both moving toward a more dynamic approach to working with neighborhood groups, and the contribution of the settlement in fostering the development and use of the group work method is clearly evidenced.

D. To Prevent Juvenile Delinquency

1. *Neighborhood Councils*

The general perspective which Frederic M. Thrasher proposed from his study of 1,300 gangs in Chicago was that "the gang and its problems constitute merely one of many symptoms of the more or less general disorganization incident to rapid economic development and the ingestion of vast numbers of alien workers." [15] There was still a good deal of that feverish mobility and expansion that characterized America during the industrial revolution. Social planning was necessary to counteract the effects of a disorganized social structure. Economy demanded, said Thrasher, that "the emphasis be shifted to the process of prevention, which attacks the roots of crime in those areas of the community which are known to be crime-breeding centers." [16]

He presented six points as prerequisites for a successful program: (1) concentration of responsibility for the function of crime prevention; (2) the program must be based upon social research; (3) there must be an integration of the services of all appropriate agencies with reference to each individual case involving a child, a family, or a gang; (4) the preventive program must be applied systematically to all children in the delinquency area of the local community; (5) new agencies must be created where it has been demonstrated by research based on special investigation and experience that the existing facilities are inadequate; (6) the public must be kept informed and educated to support the program.

Thrasher believed that the trend was toward crime prevention as a function incidental to local community plan-

[15] Thrasher, Frederic M., *The Gang* (2nd Rev. ed.), Chicago: University of Chicago Press, 1936, p. 487.
[16] *Ibid.*, p. 552.

ning, undertaken by a comprehensive local council of
community agencies. He maintained that the council of
social agencies serving the delinquency area for which a
crime prevention program was being formulated should
assume responsibility for it, since the council would be representative of most of the agencies which must cooperate in
putting the program into practical operation.[17] Thrasher suggested the creation of a committee or section of the council
which would employ an executive with a small but capable
staff "for performing the essential crime-preventing functions." [18] He pointed to the Cincinnati Social Unit Experiment and other demonstrations in the prevention of disease
and the promotion of public health, as the way in which the
principles of crime prevention could be established.

Several reasons were given for selecting the neighborhood
as the unit of a crime-prevention program by the New York
State Crime Commission in its report:

(1) the neighborhood encompasses the life of the growing de-
linquent child; (2) it includes all the primary agencies which
influence child life—the home, the school, the street, the recreation centers, the gang; (3) excessive juvenile delinquency and
habitual criminality have their roots in well-defined neighborhood areas, described by experts as interstitial areas, and col-
loquially known as slums.[19]

The Sub-Commission on Causes of the New York State Crime
Commission recommended the setting up of neighborhood
councils under the auspices of community-wide councils of
social agencies as a means of eliminating chaos in neighborhood welfare activities. The membership would consist of
neighborhood businessmen, social workers, professional men,

---

[17] See Crime Commission of New York State, *Crime and the Community:
A Study of Trends in Crime Prevention by the Sub-Commission on Causes
and Effects of Crime*, Albany: J. B. Lyon Co., 1930.

[18] *Op. cit.*, p. 539.

[19] Crime Commission of New York State, *op. cit.*, p. 174.

political leaders, and representatives of public services. Their concern would be the present and future needs of the neighborhood, based on fact finding, and their job would be to integrate all of the forces working for social welfare within the neighborhood into a harmonious program. It was recommended that each neighborhood council, as a visible sign of its integrative force, should be housed in permanent quarters where certain of the local branches of welfare agencies could also have their headquarters and that it should be under the direction of a trained executive aided by an adequate staff. In areas where there was a great deal of juvenile delinquency—and these would always be areas where other problems such as health, housing, and family rehabilitation were urgent—a section of the neighborhood council should be primarily concerned with integrating all neighborhood forces valuable for a program of crime prevention and for promoting the creation of agencies for this purpose where none exist. Since crime prevention could not be made a self-supporting program, it was recommended that wherever possible, this aspect of the neighborhood council's work be financed out of public funds.[20]

2. *Area Projects*

Another form of neighborhood approach to the prevention of juvenile delinquency is exemplified by the Chicago Area Project. It arose out of studies conducted by the Department of Sociology of the Institute of Juvenile Research. Beginning as a small project to test some of the implications and principles of these studies, it was incorporated in 1934 as a nonprofit corporation under a board of directors, with the hope that public opinion would support its financing through some public or private agency. The primary aim and chief criterion of the success or failure of the project was the

[20] *Ibid.*, p. 178.

organization of the local neighborhood to deal effectively with its own problems.

For more than four decades there had been a consistently high proportion of delinquents in certain low-income areas of Chicago. The study of the movement of different nationalities through the deteriorated areas of the city suggested a rather unimportant relationship between the volume of delinquency and nationality, but a high correlation with residence in these communities which had been traditionally characterized by crime and delinquency.[21] The crime rate of a given nationality increased as it lived in the deteriorated areas around the Loop and the industrial sections, but as it prospered, accommodated itself, and established residence in "conventional residential communities" removed from such deteriorated areas, fewer of its children found their way into the juvenile court and subsequent careers of crime. A community tradition of delinquency and crime seemed to have grown up in the deteriorated areas.

The essential purpose of the Area Project became one of discovering the pertinent social processes and significant cultural organization of the community as expressed in the institutions of local residents themselves, and through these to introduce values consistent with the standards of "conventional society." It sought to discover by actual demonstration and measurement a procedure for the treatment of delinquents and the prevention of delinquency in those neighborhoods. The program's main feature was the emphasis it placed on the participation of the residents of the neighborhood in its planning and operation. Although certain changes could not take place in local neighborhoods except as part of general changes in the social order, the project sought to

[21] Burgess, Ernest W., Lohman, Joseph D., and Shaw, Clifford R., "The Chicago Area Project," *Yearbook of the National Probation Association, 1937,* New York: National Probation Association, 1937, p. 20.

determine what constructive changes could be effected in the environment to reduce the volume of delinquency. The residents were provided facilities and professional guidance for the development of their own programs for their own children. An effort was made to move away from the traditional methods of charity to a point where the people themselves had a prominent part in studying community problems, formulating goals, determining policies, and operating program activities. In each area the planning and management of the program was the responsibility of a committee of from 100 to 500 representative local citizens. The work was carried on through subcommittees.

The project operated on the theory that the natural leadership of a community, a product of its distinctive life, could be strategically utilized in giving direction of a constructive nature to the cultural and recreational life of the community. The kinds of activities carried on by the project were in the main the same as those offered by the YMCA, the YWCA, the settlements, and boys' clubs. However, the program was developed for the neighborhood as a whole rather than for a part of it. Control was vested in the actual residents of the neighborhood, instead of in lay and professional persons residing in or representing the interests of more privileged communities. Instead of using professionally trained leaders, local neighborhood people were recruited and trained. Maximum use was made of established neighborhood institutions, especially such natural social groupings as churches, societies, and clubs. This policy was felt to be preferable to creating new institutions embodying the values and sentiments of the more "conventional" communities. The activities program of the area project was regarded primarily as a device for enlisting the active participation of local residents in a constructive community enterprise, and for creating and crystallizing neighborhood sentiment to promote the welfare of children and the social and physical improvement of the community as a whole. Some of its results are discussed in the next chapter.

E. The Coordinating Council Movement

1. *Origin and Scope*

As the area project had sought to prevent juvenile delinquency, so did the coordinating council. Differing from the area project in method, it sought initially to achieve its goal by bringing together representatives of organizations through which individual attention could be given to children who were developing behavior problems leading to delinquency. In 1933 the Probation Department of Los Angeles County and the Juvenile Court began to develop coordinating councils, each of which had three committees: Adjustment, Character Building, and Environment. The pattern followed had been developed 15 years earlier by August Vollmer, police chief of Berkeley, California. From 1933 to 1936 sixty councils were developed in Los Angeles County.[22]

Although the most widespread development of coordinating councils to prevent juvenile delinquency was in California, councils were also organized in other parts of the country. Stimulation came from various national sources. One of these was the National Advisory Committee on Coordinating Councils, organized in December, 1934, at the time of the Attorney General's Conference on Crime.[23] Another source of the stimulation was the Annual Conference of the National Probation Association in 1936 where ques-

---

[22] Scudder, Kenyon J., "The Co-ordinating Council at Work," *Yearbook of the National Probation Association, 1936,* New York: National Probation Association, 1936, p. 68.

[23] Beam, Kenneth S., "Community Coordination—National Survey," *Yearbook of the National Probation Association, 1937,* New York: National Probation Association, 1937, p. 70.

tions were raised concerning the objectives of coordinating and neighborhood councils. These questions included: should the prevention of delinquency be their major objective, or should they seek to improve any condition in the community affecting the lives of children? What should be the relationship of the neighborhood council to the council of social agencies? What agency should sponsor coordinating or neighborhood councils? Who should be the national sponsor?

A number of attempts were made to consolidate effort at the national level to give leadership to this movement. At the first National Conference on Coordinating Councils, held in 1936, plans were being formulated to bring together the heads of national organizations whose local units participated in coordinating and neighborhood councils to formulate a policy for the guidance of their local units. It was also resolved that in arranging the program for the 1937 conference the possibility of cooperation with the community organization section of the National Conference of Social Work should be considered.[24] Meetings to this end were held. The National Social Work Council which was asked to assume national sponsorship of the community council movement, appointed a National Committee on Community Coordination consisting of representatives of national social work organizations to take over the work of the National Advisory Committee on Coordinating Councils.[25] In 1937 the National Conference on Community Coordination asked the National Probation Association to continue studying, compiling, and distributing information on the developments in this field and to continue to give assistance to communities desiring the service.

[24] "The First National Conference on Coordinating Councils," *Yearbook of the National Probation Association, 1936,* New York: National Probation Association, 1936, p. 117.

[25] Beam, *op. cit.,* pp. 71-72.

2. *Extent of the Movement*

In 1936 Kenneth Beam, special field agent of the National Probation Association, carried out a survey of those councils which brought together representatives of public and private agencies and citizens' groups (or some combination of these three) for studying and improving those influences which shape the lives of children and youth. He followed up this survey with others in 1937 and 1938 which provide us with some interesting data on this movement.

The coordinating or neighborhood council was a cross between a council of social agencies and a community council of the type developed after World War I. It was like the council of social agencies in that it included representatives of social agencies in its membership and worked through the agencies wherever possible; it was like the community council in that it was organized on a neighborhood basis and included local citizens in its membership. During the first years of the depression, social workers took the initiative in creating neighborhood councils to talk over with local residents some of the problems connected with the administration of relief. As the emergency relief situation subsided many of these councils went out of existence, while others took on new objectives and continued to flourish. Publicity on the juvenile delinquency situation led directly to the organization of many new councils.

Most of the councils which put major emphasis on delinquency prevention began with a survey of juvenile delinquency and virtually all took steps to improve recreation facilities. Some councils were successful in getting a community center for the neighborhood, either by utilizing some building already there, or through the construction of a new building. Some councils were instrumental in organizing community chests.

The 1936 survey showed that there were more than 250

councils in 163 cities and towns in 20 states. Before 1935 councils were organized in 95 cities and towns in 12 states. During 1935 new councils were organized in 43 cities and towns, bringing to 19 the total of represented states.[26] Over 300 local councils reported in 1937. This meant that 50 more were listed, not necessarily that 50 more had been organized. Kenneth Beam reported between 350 and 380 coordinating councils for 1938 in 29 states. Most of these were in states and cities where this work had been going on for some time.

From his surveys Beam believed that one of the prerequisites of success was sponsorship by a reliable agency—public or private. For counties or large cities he advocated a central executive board representing the public and private agencies, the citizens' groups concerned with children and youth, and the local neighborhood councils.[27] In this way the agencies would have a part in planning the movement and would know what all the local councils were doing. The local councils would have the cooperation of the agencies and would be in a better position to improve services. If a public department sponsored a group of councils it could create a board made up of other departments and private agencies. According to the report of the 1937 survey a number of state governments were active in stimulating and sponsoring community councils. The Washington Department of Social Security (mentioned above) and the Illinois Department of Public Welfare employed executives for this purpose. The California Department of Education agreed to sponsor the movement in that state and expected to have a field worker. About 200 of the 300 councils received some kind of help from public or private agencies outside their neighborhoods. Many of the councils in the remaining 100 instances had the

[26] Beam, Kenneth S., "Community Coordination for Prevention of Delinquency (Report of a National Survey)," *Yearbook of the National Probation Association, 1936*, New York: National Probation Association, 1936, pp. 89-90.
[27] Beam, *op. cit.,* p. 108.

backing of some local organization which had taken the initiative in getting them started.

The great majority of coordinating councils had no budget. The Stockyards Council in Chicago received $5,000 a year from the meat packing firms in the district. The Community Service Council at Hastings-on-Hudson in 1936 secured $6,000 from tax funds. Many councils benefited from federal projects under the Civil Works Administration, Emergency Relief Administration, Works Progress Administration, and the National Youth Administration. The costliest item, staff service, was usually borne by the sponsoring organization.

It was Beam's contention that field workers were necessary. He conceived of the field worker as a liaison between the central planning board and the local council, who represented the central board at local council meetings and advised local councils on methods.[28] Throughout his three surveys Beam noted a steady increase in the number of staff persons serving councils. Councils of social agencies provided more staff than any other type of sponsorship. They not only sponsored the councils but provided employed personnel to assist them. Few attempts were made to organize neighborhood councils without a trained field worker. Most of the newly organized councils reported in the 1938 survey were in cities where full-time staff was available.

One of the questions asked in the 1938 survey was: "What are some of the major problems faced by the council?" There were 173 answers received from 19 states. Nearly all the questionnaires were filled out by the council chairmen. Among community conditions constituting the most serious problems were: housing conditions, relief, unemployment, health hazards, liquor, the breakdown of families, gambling, undesirable commercial recreation, traffic hazards, and un-

[28] Beam, Kenneth S., "Community Coordination—National Survey," *Yearbook of the National Probation Association, 1937,* New York: National Probation Association, 1937, p. 65.

regulated street trades. Recreation facilities received almost as much attention as all the above combined. Problems of organization included: agency-minded leaders; lack of co-operation on the part of public officials, school administrators, and the courts; the need of cooperation between adult and youth organizations; the integration of lay and professional interests; and the general problems of bringing together the diverse interests of the community. Of 57 councils listing problems of organization, 33 mentioned the problem of securing cooperation from officials and heads of agencies. Councils without a paid executive mentioned the need for one and tended to be concerned mainly with problems of administration. Councils with a paid executive focused attention more upon the problems of the community.[29]

Over the period of Beam's three surveys there was a noticeable shift in emphasis from delinquency prevention to an interest in all children, and towards the general objective of making the community a more wholesome place in which to live.

Strict adherence to the coordinating function was stressed by Beam. The council should be a medium for the discovery of needs and conditions in the community and for planning to meet the needs and change the conditions. The council itself should not attempt to offer direct service which should be the responsibility of the organizations represented on it.

F. The Neighborhood Approach to Community Planning

1. *By Councils of Social Agencies*

In this period many councils of social agencies sponsored projects in neighborhood organization in an effort to increase their effectiveness through a neighborhood or district ap-

[29] Beam, Kenneth S., "Coordinating Council Progress—National Survey," *Yearbook of the National Probation Association, 1938,* New York: National Probation Association, 1938, pp. 313-315.

proach. As shown in the surveys made by Kenneth Beam neighborhood councils, to be successful, needed sponsorship and needed to be related to the network of social services. The specific purposes for which councils of social agencies undertook to use the neighborhood approach varied as did the methods and results. An analysis of efforts made in Hartford, Detroit, Syracuse, and Pittsburgh will serve to illustrate.[30]

In Hartford, as a result of the community survey of 1934, it was decided to develop neighborhood "units" to focus and coordinate the services of city-wide agencies in certain neighborhoods. It was hoped thereby to make the social services more readily available in family situations where problems were developing. The structure of the Lawrence Street Unit, organized in July 1935, was worked out by committees of the Council of Social Agencies and jointly approved by the Council's Executive Committee and the Board of Directors of Mitchell House, a settlement in the area which served as official headquarters of the unit. The settlement and the Council agreed that they were looking toward the development of a committee or council of neighborhood citizens which would give neighborhood backing to the social service program. The Head Resident of Mitchell House became secretary of the unit and served as staff member of the Council of Social Agencies, for which she received financial compensation. The unit had two subcommittees. The Policy Committee, consisting of one board member and the executive of each of the 23 agencies serving the area, discussed service to the area. The Neighborhood Case Council, made up of professional workers representing various agencies,

[30] The following sources have been drawn upon extensively for the material of this section:

   The Neighborhood Approach to Community Planning, Community Chests and Councils, Inc., Bulletin No. 94, New York, 1937. *Fifteen Years of Community Council Development*, A Report Presented at the Evaluation Committee Meeting of the Association of Community Councils of Pittsburgh and Allegheny County, June, 1946.

discussed specific cases and general problems of the neighborhood related to the work of the participating agencies. Mitchell House, which for ten years had provided services or secured these through other agencies, engaged a case worker to develop a central file of information on families in the neighborhood. It became, in effect, a central intake service for the neighborhood. The unit was closely related to the functional divisions of the Council of Social Agencies and eventually came under the control of the Council.

In Detroit there was a need for interpreting the functions and services of the rapidly expanding Department of Public Welfare. Towards the end of 1931 the Metropolitan Secretary for Branches of the Council of Social Agencies began to organize the whole city of Detroit into 13 districts, corresponding with the district organization of the department. The Council already had eight branches in incorporated suburbs that were a part of the metropolitan area, and four of these had local secretaries. The 13 districts were not "neighborhoods" having any geographic or cultural tradition of unity, nor were the councils set up primarily for the coordination of services. Each of the local groups developed its own objectives. They held educational meetings, acted as pressure groups, and to some extent coordinated services. Membership was on an individual basis, and although there were no organizational memberships the majority of the members came from the social agencies and the schools. Between the district councils and the Executive Committee of the Council of Social Agencies stood the Central Committee, made up of public agency officials and representatives of district councils. Staff service to the district councils, which was provided by the Council of Social Agencies in the same way as to its own functional divisions, was discontinued in 1933 due to lack of finances. When it was resumed in November of 1934 only three of the 13 councils were found to have any formal organization.

In Syracuse the West Side Neighborhood Council was organized to help reduce delinquency and to improve child life in the area. It held educational meetings and took action as a pressure group. It sought the participation of lay residents of the neighborhood rather than of professionals. Any individual could identify himself with the Council; agencies as such did not become members. Out of its work there developed a "Neighborhood House" in which its meetings were held and where several agencies had their offices. There was a tendency toward coordination of services and a beginning of central intake and referral procedures. The project was not tied in with any operating program of service in the area. Staff service was furnished by the Council of Social Agencies, whose Executive Committee had final control over the project. As in the case of Detroit, there was an intermediary committee called the Advisory Committee on Neighborhood Councils whose purpose was to interest key public and private agency people in the project.

Developments in Pittsburgh were more extensive and of longer duration than in the other cities described. The emergency situation in the administration of relief in 1931 prompted the Federation of Social Agencies of Pittsburgh and Allegheny County to call a meeting at which it was decided that, under the joint sponsorship of the Federation of Social Agencies, the Welfare Fund, and the Allegheny County Emergency Association, community councils would be established. Through these councils it was hoped that representatives of all organizations concerned might together explore the extent of the need in their area, list the available resources, and plan the most effective use of relief and other social services. Pittsburgh was divided into 18 districts. In each of these, organization meetings were held to which representatives were invited from various local organizations as well as representatives of the social agencies and other city-wide organizations concerned with the relief crisis. In a month's time councils were organized in 16 districts and under way in the remaining two. Although each worked out its own constitution there was a tendency to set up the same kinds of committees. In September 1932 all 18 councils had committees on relief, 15 had committees on housing, and 16 had committees on recreation. For each of these activities there was a city-wide committee consisting of the local committee chairmen. The Central Council was composed of the chairmen of the 18 districts, the chairmen of city-wide committees, the executives of city-wide agencies concerned with the situation, and six representatives from each of the boards of the Welfare Fund, the Emergency Association, and the Federation of Social Agencies. By February of 1934 there were 22 councils organized in the County. In addition to handling a large number of inquiries and complaints concerning the distribution of relief, the councils offered certain direct services, particularly recreational services. In co-operation with group work agencies and the various work relief projects, many of the councils, with the help of volunteer leadership established community centers. In the years 1935-1936, after the emergency period had passed, community councils gave much less attention to offering direct services but sought rather to stimulate existing agencies to offer the direct services the councils felt were needed. In the course of the Pittsburgh Social Study of 1936, two types of community councils were found among the eight city councils examined. The first type was the neighborhood council of social agencies, in which staff members of various social agencies constituted the greater part of the council and its committees. The second type was located in small communities where there were few social agencies and tended to enlist representation from lay groups and to have members-at-large. The county community councils were of this second type.

Although from the beginning the Federation of Social Agencies had sponsored the community councils, the staff was provided from work relief rolls and group work agencies. The Federation had five field secretaries by the fall of 1934. For a period of years, staff members of group work agencies continued to give service to local councils. The mixture of motives among the sponsoring organizations was reflected in the work of the councils. This was one of the weaknesses of having agencies initiate local councils. The Report of the Pittsburgh Social Study revealed insufficient cooperation among the agencies and the lack of any policy-forming board for the councils. As a result, the Board of the Federation in 1936 appointed an Advisory Committee on Community Councils consisting of representatives of the various city-wide agencies and of the individual community councils. It was to formulate policy and to serve as a clearinghouse on council projects. The Joint Committee on Community Councils, set up by the Community Fund and the Federation of Social Agencies, recommended in 1938 that the Federation continue to give field service to the councils recognizing their autonomy and that consultation staff service on community councils be available to groups desiring it. It was recognized that community councils had been effective in bringing about informed consideration of local problems and action on them. As a result of these recommendations, in November 1938 the Advisory Committee and the individual local councils moved to establish the Association of Community Councils consisting of two representatives of each active community council, to function as a voluntary, cooperative association of autonomous community councils. It was to concern itself with city-wide problems to strengthen the programs of the individual councils through cooperative effort and when necessary to coordinate activities. In addition to representatives of councils, the Association included representatives from city-wide social agencies and representatives-at-large not connected with social agencies.

2. *Some Significant Factors*

In each of the examples cited the council of social agencies was interested in arousing neighborhood participation through a better understanding of the services available and the needs to be met and through taking an active part in meeting them. There were differences in the degree of coordination of services attempted at the neighborhood level. In Hartford and Pittsburgh some social agencies lent their sponsorship to community councils along with that of the councils of social agencies. Pittsburgh's experience indicated the advisability of agencies withdrawing from sponsorship in favor of participating in councils on the same basis as other agencies and organizations. It is also interesting to note that the neighborhood councils cut down on direct service in favor of stimulating the existing agencies to provide the services.

There was considerable variety in the forms of neighborhood organization. Some were associations of individuals while others were interorganizational bodies. Where the emphasis was on individual membership, council activity seemed to be focused on the educational effects of attending meetings, participating in committees and taking action to get more service for the area. This was particularly true of Detroit and Syracuse. In Hartford this kind of citizen support was sought for the more specific purpose of better coordination of service to families in the area. The development of interorganizational councils at the neighborhood level was the trend in Pittsburgh. Some tended to be neighborhood councils of social agencies, while others were made up of representatives of citizen groups and members-at-large.

In all but one of the cities the council of social agencies had some kind of intermediary committee on neighborhood organization between the neighborhood councils and the board of the council of social agencies. This device made it possible for the councils of social agencies to develop broad policy on neighborhood councils and in some cases provided an opportunity for representatives of neighborhood councils to come together to discuss their common problems. The development in Pittsburgh of an Association of Community Councils seemed to indicate the values of a large measure of participation of neighborhood council representatives in working out of policy.

The provision of staff service by the council of social agencies was needed, not only to sustain a close relationship between the council of social agencies and the neighborhood councils, but also to help neighborhood councils function adequately. This did not seem to contradict the need of neighborhood councils for self-determination.

In looking back over this period we see adaptations of neighborhood organization to the conditions of the great depression and a rapid increase in the number of community councils. The federations or councils of social agencies that were being developed at the city-wide level often fostered the development of neighborhood or district councils. As we shall see, this pattern persisted and developed further.

CHAPTER V

NEIGHBORHOOD ORGANIZATION FOR COMMUNITY WELFARE

A. World War II and After

1. *Wartime Needs and Services*

During World War II there were large-scale shifts of population. Over 10,000,000 young men left their homes for military service. Young men and women, even whole families moved to industrial cities and new war production centers to undertake the thousands of new jobs that had to be done. Some 20,000,000 persons, including children of all ages, moved to war centers. Some people left peace time employment, while many others who had been dependent upon public assistance became for the first time gainfully employed in industry. Many thousands of workers were subject to the topsy-turvy life of shift work. A large number of women were employed, doing what used to be "man's work." Many of them were mothers, whose children had to be cared for while they were at work. Family life frequently suffered from the father's being in the service and the mother's working, which left the children virtually without parents. Youngsters were growing up more quickly than before. Some 3,000,000 teen-age youth were employed.[1] Adolescents, just out of school, were finding themselves suddenly financially independent and somewhat unprepared for this condition.

Special services were needed to help individuals and families through these dislocations—day care for children of working mothers; recreational opportunities for all, with special stress on shift workers and those in the armed forces; emergency housing projects; special leisure-time and counseling services for teen-agers; vocational counseling, special programs of job training and retraining.

Because these predicaments represented obstacles to a maximum war effort there was a united and over-all approach to the problems which also characterized the response in support of the services needed. Citizen participation in the efforts to meet these needs reached a new high. The demands of the emergency brought thousands of citizens into the work of the Red Cross, salvage collections, air raid precautions, defense councils, and numerous other projects. This wartime experience brought many individuals into community activity and led many organizations for the first time to work together for the common welfare. This had a telling effect, not only upon individual citizens and civic organizations, but also upon community organization for education, health, welfare, and recreation.

2. *Effect of Defense Councils*

Civilian defense brought some form of joint activity into every part of the country. Although some defense councils manifested little interest in social welfare problems, in others both the citizens and the agencies were very much concerned with these matters. The defense council, as an official operation of local, state, and federal governments, involved local

[1] *The Road to Community Reorganization,* New York: The Woman's Foundation, 1945, p. 11.

government in social welfare planning. It was said that health and welfare planning was becoming more of a citizens' movement and less a mere federation of operating agencies.[2] This was not a matter of lessening participation by agencies or doing away with agency memberships. It was rather a matter of looking beyond the agencies and departments of government to the citizens who ultimately are the ones to support and use the services. A greater degree of citizen participation in social planning was developing. In Syracuse, New York, a study made in 1942 revealed that 70 per cent of all the families in Onondaga County received one or more direct health, welfare, or group work services, with the average being two services per family.[3] The broader support and wider distribution of the social services has provided the basis for more extensive citizen participation in community organization for social welfare.

3. *Serving People in Neighborhoods*

In a report on the reorganization of community services (education, health, recreation, and welfare) issued by the Woman's Foundation in 1945 stress was laid on the concept that "the welfare of all the people is the concern of all the people." [4] The report, the product of lay and professional social welfare leaders, urged that full advantage be taken of the experience of wartime organizations, among which it listed the neighborhood work of some of the local civilian defense units. Attention was directed to the extension of neighborhood center programs in the public schools. Community service centers or information and referral centers were advocated as a means whereby citizens could get information about available services. In urban areas, district

[2] Ford, Lyman S., "The Effect of World War II on Community Organization for Health and Welfare," *Proceedings of the National Conference of Social Work, 1944,* New York: Columbia University Press, 1944, p. 396.
[3] *Ibid.,* p. 397.
[4] *The Road to Community Reorganization, op. cit.,* p. 10.

offices were recommended for bringing services closer to people in their own neighborhoods.[5]

An increasing number of community, district, area, and neighborhood councils helped bring people and services together. These were organized for defense, for youth, for recreation, for adult education, and for many other special as well as general purposes. Some of these were under the auspices of public agencies or departments; others were sponsored by settlements or adult education organizations. One of the most significant trends was the increasing number of local neighborhood councils that became affiliated with or developed out of the efforts of city-wide social welfare planning bodies. Councils of social agencies found that neighborhood councils were a vital part of an over-all planning council. They cut across the lines of functional divisions and focused attention on the interrelatedness of social problems. They reached out to the broad citizen constituency of social work; they helped to keep the focus on the purposes of particular services, the needs they sought to meet, and the people served.

A questionnaire circulated by Community Chests and Councils, Inc., to its member councils in 1946, revealed that there were neighborhood councils in at least 50 cities, and that in most of these the city-wide welfare council was giving staff service to neighborhood councils. The affiliation of these neighborhood councils with the over-all social planning bodies have had interesting effects on the city-wide organizations. The growing interest in neighborhood organization on the part of community welfare councils (or councils of social agencies) seemed to signify a broadening of function and practice.

[5] *Ibid.*, pp. 22-23.

B. Defense Councils

1. *Purpose and Scope*

The Office of Civilian Defense was set up in 1941 to facilitate cooperation with state and local governments on measures for the protection of the civilian population in emergency periods, to facilitate civilian participation in the defense program, and to aid in sustaining national morale. The situation differed from that of World War I partly by virtue of the great increase in community resources. Practically all the service clubs and veterans' organizations had come into being after the first World War as had many social agencies, community chests, councils of social agencies, coordinating, community, and neighborhood councils. In 1941 there was a large number of organizations in existence for carrying on normal services and for assuming necessary additional responsibilities.

Recreation, health, welfare, housing, and other problems had a national importance and a local impact that were widely recognized. But councils of national defense were not set up to deal with all phases of these problems. State and local councils were to confine their attention solely to defense programs and not to extend their interests to normal programs of public, quasi-public, or private agencies unless they impinged directly on matters of defense.

Many questions were raised regarding the relation of neighborhood and coordinating councils to the defense council program. It was generally agreed that existing councils should not be designated as official defense councils, but that practical working relationships should be developed with defense councils wherever they existed.

Every state made provision for the development of defense councils. More than 11,000 local councils were established under the provisions of existing legislation, new legislation, or executive order of the governors, and the stimulation of state defense or war councils.[6] Not all of these were effective, but a good many were. These community councils were co-operative planning bodies exercising no authority over any department or agency. Their effectiveness came from the pooling of information, from joint discussion of problems and programs, and from the development of joint recommendations to one or more agencies or departments.

2. *Block Organization*

In some cities the Office of Civilian Defense had a block plan. It was usually set up on a territorial basis but was sometimes combined with the organization of committees for special purposes, or with the organization of a council based on special interests.

In Nashville, Tennessee, for example, the Central Volunteer Bureau, which was a committee of the Local Defense Council as well as a permanent activity of the Council of Community Agencies, worked out a block plan of organization. Its purpose was to develop community consciousness, neighborliness, and responsibility for the community welfare so that any emergency could be met. The city and outlying areas were divided into 20 districts, on the basis of census tract divisions. Responsibility for each district was assigned to a women's organization. A block committee of three to five members from its own membership was appointed by the leader of each organization. This committee elected a chairman and other officers as needed, added members, set up subcommittees, studied the district, and appointed a block leader in each block. The block leaders were to gather in-

---

[6] U. S. Office of Civilian Defense, *The Community Council—A Natural Outgrowth of the Defense Council,* Washington: Government Printing Office, 1945, p. 1.

formation and be ready to carry out the requests of the district chairman.[7]

There were various forms of such local organization, more and less democratic. Some of these laid the foundations for the establishment of community councils.

3. Retaining Wartime Gains

In some parts of the country the entire machinery of the Office of Civilian Defense was retained for peacetime operation. In 90 Tennessee communities the Citizens' Service Corps, originally set up to meet emergency needs, were retained as permanent community councils.[8]

The Office of Civilian Defense urged several principles for consideration in retaining wartime gains.[9] These suggested that: the community council should be part of local government, established by local ordinance and with an administrative budget provided at least in part from tax funds; government should be the agency to bring all local organizations together; by including a community council in the structure of local government, citizens could participate in local government, not only at election time, but all year round. Decisions on the important community developments are of concern to a number of interdependent areas of planning—economic, physical, and social. The council should be representative of the major agencies, and important community groups. Since a planning organization that operates a program tends to neglect its over-all planning function neither the council nor its committees should operate programs. For instance, recreation committees which undertook to operate

[7] "Nashville, Tenn., Block Plan of Organization for Defense," *Community Coordination*, September-October, 1941, pp. 10-11. See later sections of this chapter, especially Adult Education.

[8] McClusky, Howard Y., "Some Current Trends in Community Organization," *Adult Education Bulletin*, X, February, 1946, p. 72.

[9] U. S. Office of Civilian Defense, *op. cit.*

recreation centers for servicemen soon became so involved in the problems of operating the centers that they devoted little attention to planning for the recreation needs of servicemen, immigrant war workers and their families. Community councils might, however, operate such common services as a volunteer office, fact-finding or research, and publicity services. It was suggested that the operation of these common services should be delegated to a committee so that the efforts of the council would not be diverted from its broad planning functions. The community council should not duplicate or supplant well-established community planning or coordinating bodies. It was recognized that the effectiveness of community organization is largely dependent upon the skill of the executive staff.

Many of these conclusions, drawn from the experience of the defense councils, reflect trends and principles which may be observed in other developments. The rapid expansion of the public social services and the sponsorship of neighborhood councils by public agencies, described in a later section of this chapter, may be pointing in the direction of tax-supported community planning councils for health and welfare services.

The need for separate auspices for direct service and for the coordinating function and the significance of community councils as coordinating bodies, will be developed later in this chapter.

C. Education

1. *Wartime Community Programs*

During World War II, and in the period following, advocates of the adult education movement showed great interest in community councils. This came about through the tremendous increase in adult education activities, especially in the planning of programs on a community-wide scale. This high degree of interest in community organization was partly due to the development of defense councils, campaigns for the sale of war service bonds, the organization of USO councils, and so forth, to mobilize greater participation in the war effort. It was due also to the activity of community groups concerned with juvenile delinquency, racial prejudice, adjustment of veterans and war workers. As a result, in many communities adult education councils were revived or initiated. Where there was no over-all social planning council, a general community council was sometimes organized.

One wartime example of an adult education program with a community organization focus was found in Chicago. When the Morale Department of the Metropolitan Chicago Office of Civilian Defense developed a program of public discussions at the block level, the Adult Education Council of Chicago was assigned responsibility for the administrative and technical requirements of the program.[10] The city was divided into seven areas. Within each of these divisions there were from 11 to 25 distinct communities—a total of 108 for the city. Each of the divisions had a division chief and a division commander responsible for the planning and organization of civilian defense programs in their areas. Each division chief appointed a division morale officer one of whose responsibilities was to give practical expression to the requirements of a public discussion program. The division morale chairmen appointed community morale chairmen to assist in carrying out the program in the communities. The actual operation of the program was left to the block.[11] In most of the 15,000 blocks of the city a block captain was elected by the block residents. The Adult Education Council gave field service in the programs of the blocks and in the training of discussion leaders.

[10] McCallister, R. and Luke, R. A., "Chicago Block Discussion Program," *Adult Education Journal*, II, October, 1943, pp. 170-172.
[11] *Ibid.*, p. 170.

2. School and Community

After the War there was widespread interest throughout the country in building community centers as living war memorials. Many such plans conceived of a combination school and community center, often including provision for an active and representative committee of citizens.

The basic idea was not new, as we know from the history of earlier periods. It came to the fore again as a result of wartime experience in which the schools took on many new responsibilities and carried them for the duration of the war. The War Production Training Program, nursery schools, day care were some of these responsibilities. This was in line with modern educational philosophy which recognizes that "the school is the one institution touching all parts of the social fabric that is capable of serving as this focal point of unification." [12]

In addition to nationwide activities, in some communities the school was made the center for all types of major community improvement activities—health, recreation, community planning, and marketing and production cooperatives. In smaller communities the school tended to become the center of community life more readily than in the cities. However, the problem of trying to divide the larger metropolitan communities into smaller centers of neighborhood living gave expression to the idea of a community school even in the heart of the largest cities. In the opinion of some writers, the successful discharge of these added responsibilities demonstrated the soundness of placing the responsibility for over-all planning and provision for the youth of any community in the hands of the school administration. [13]

[12] Hunt, H. C. and Leonard, J. P., "Participation in Community Coordination and Planning," *Forty-fifth Yearbook of the National Society for the Study of Education, 1946,* Chicago: Society for the Study of Education, 1946, Part II, p. 86.
[13] *Ibid.,* pp. 87-88.

This point of view was exemplified to some extent in a development in Oakland, California. The Committee on Juvenile Delinquency of the Council of Social Agencies persuaded the Oakland Public Schools to sponsor the development of neighborhood community councils as part of its school-centered recreation program. The School Department, as a public agency used universally by the community, was regarded as being in a position to pull together effectively such community services as the churches, Boy Scouts, Girl Scouts, YMCA, YWCA, boys' clubs, city recreation department, police department, and housing authority.[14] This was a rather exceptional instance. In most communities the over-all planning and coordination of health, welfare, and recreation services continued to be carried on by the councils of social agencies.

3. Adult Education and Community Organization

Some adult education leaders have used the term "community organization" loosely, applying it to various processes of group life and, among other things, considering it as a vehicle of adult education. It has sometimes been regarded as a means of access to a large number of adults whom it would be difficult to reach via other avenues of approach because of the cleavages of race and social stratification. It has also been regarded as a means for the mobilization of community resources to meet human need. In this sense, community organization is a method that applies at various levels from the neighborhood to the nation as a whole.

Some people claimed for adult education the same kind of functional responsibility for community organization that others claimed for the settlement in the "neighborhood." It was felt that adult education should have as one of its major goals the planned coordination of community efforts, since

[14] *Inter-Council Newsletter,* New York: Institute of Adult Education, Teachers College, Columbia University, April, 1944, p. 6.

adult education seeks to further the practice of democracy. Cooperative activity of community groups directed toward the solution of common problems was considered as democracy in action. Therefore, by helping this process along, adult education could further democratic practice.

Adult education methods have been used by various types of agencies and organizations. Educators have felt the field of social work moving closer to the field of education as the social worker in community organization has sought to mobilize the resources of the community to meet need. Social work has set up programs in community organization virtually identical with those of adult education. On the other hand the adult education council in smaller communities has in fact often functioned as a community welfare council.

Following the war there was a rising demand all over the country for cooperative planning and action at the local level. In the field of adult education this was reflected by emphasis on the "community approach to adult education." The State of Michigan set up a Community Adult Education Section within its State University Extension Division. The New York State Citizens' Council and the State Department of Education's Bureau of Adult Education emphasized strengthening the role of the local community. Councils of social agencies, such as those in New Orleans and Cleveland, set up adult education sections to coordinate existing activities and stimulate the provision of new ones. In some communities independent adult education councils were organized or revitalized.

The American Association for Adult Education set up a committee to study community organization as it related to adult education. The approach decided upon by the Committee was to discover the contributions that adult education could make to community organization. The proposal involved the preparation of case studies representative of geographic areas, communities ranging from unincorporated to metropolitan areas, single purpose councils and over-all planning bodies.[15]

The report stressed the need to find ways to offer those who live in large cities the opportunity to participate in and plan for the social well-being of their communities. It defined adult education as "the deliberate effort to facilitate learning in adults" and community organization as "the dynamic balancing of community needs and resources." [16] The study attempted to identify the skills required in community organization by examining the processes of community organization in the light of the processes of adult education. As a conclusion from its case studies the report stated that adult education can contribute to community organization in four major areas: identification of needs, identification of resources, leader training, and development of community readiness.

The work of the adult educators in this study was hampered by the lack of definition of community organization processes. Until more extensive analysis of community organization practice gives us a framework within which to define community organization processes there will continue to be grave difficulties in the way of those who seek to contribute to the development of this process.

D. Settlements

1. *Meeting Neighborhood Needs*

Settlement leaders in this period warned against the evils of "living up to a building." [17] Settlements, they said, are

[15] Luke, R. A., "Committee on Community Organization: A Progress Report," *Adult Education Journal,* VI, April, 1947, pp. 76-77.

[16] *Community Education in Action—A Report on Community Organization and Adult Education,* prepared by the Committee on Community Organization of the American Association for Adult Education, New York: AAAE (through the cooperation of the Institute of Adult Education, Teachers College, Columbia University), 1948, pp. 42-43.

[17] Simkhovitch, Mary K., "Neighborhood Planning and the Settlements," *The Survey,* LXXIX, June, 1943, p. 175.

not activity centers, but centers of neighborhood initiative, experimentation, and coordination. They have always been interested in the smaller units of society—the family, the group, and the neighborhood.[18]

A new venture for settlements in adapting their resources to meet the needs of neighborhoods of a large city is to be found in the Neighborhood Settlement Association formed by three Cleveland settlements in 1948.

The Association set up a Board of Directors, two-thirds of which consisted of representatives from the three participating agencies and one-third of members-at-large representing various interests in the greater Cleveland community. Advisory Boards were set up in each of the new areas served by the Association and they in turn elected two representatives each to the Board of the Association.

The Association, which employed an Executive Director, works with the agencies in jointly determining new types of neighborhood settlement services; the final decision and responsibility rests with the Association Board. The Association establishes program standards after consultation with member agencies. Each agency is responsible for setting its own program policy using the Association staff as a consultative resource. The agencies discover areas of unmet need in adjacent locations and report them to the Association Board. The Association works with other city-wide public and voluntary agencies serving neighborhoods.

The Association participates in the planning activities of the Welfare Federation. During its first nine months of existence the major efforts of the Association were directed to setting up new group work services in the three areas designated by the Group Work Council of the Welfare Federation as being in greatest need of them.

An agency like the Neighborhood Settlement Association,

[18] Murray, Clyde E., *New Horizons for the Settlement Movement,* presidential address, Annual Conference, National Federation of Settlements, 1944, p. 3.

in offering direct service on a city-wide basis to neighborhoods needing them, can carry some of the direct-service functions that often are proposed or assumed as tasks of local community councils.

2. Neighborhood Service

The Cleveland Settlement Study, undertaken by the National Federation of Settlements at the request of the Welfare Federation of Cleveland, listed certain neighborhood services among the kinds of work that the settlement does. Neighborhood service was said to consist of (1) the program assistance which settlements give to local organizations; (2) stimulation of, or leadership in the study of, neighborhood problems in cooperation with local citizens' organizations or service agencies; (3) helping to develop good working relationships among staff workers of various agencies serving the area.[19]

By making facilities and leadership available or helping them to develop their own, program assistance to local organizations can develop the capacity of individuals and of groups to participate in activities of concern to the whole neighborhood.

The settlement has a responsibility to work with indigenous groups in the neighborhood and help create associations of neighborhood people, in order to stimulate interest in neighborhood conditions and their understanding of the wider implications of these conditions. This service should be directed toward providing the kinds of experience that will enable individuals to participate as representatives of their groups in intergroup activities in behalf of the area. Neighborhood service of this type can help develop "grassroots" leadership for participation in area councils, and in advisory and sponsoring committees for settlement programs.

[19] McDowell, John, General Report of the Cleveland Settlement Study, Cleveland: Research Department, Welfare Federation of Cleveland, 1946, pp. 18-21.

Where there is no area council the settlement may take the initiative in bringing together the staff workers of other agencies in the neighborhood. This is related to mutual efforts to improve services in the neighborhood but not to community planning for services. Although the settlement may take the initiative on such neighborhood service, the Cleveland Study states that any continuing organization which evolves should be established independently of the settlement. In this kind of neighborhood service the settlement has the same responsibility as other participating groups to point up needs that may require the services of another agency or the establishment of a new service.

Where there is an area council which provides a medium for interagency planning and for participation of citizen groups, such councils should be regarded as resources for planning and action by settlements. The report stressed the importance of settlement groups participating in projects with other groups in the community and emphasized greater participation by the neighborhood in planning and policy making for settlements. Where there is a need and a readiness for an area council it was suggested that the settlement might appropriately take the initiative in developing one.

The neighborhood service of a settlement, said the report, differs from the activities of an area council in that it consists, in the main, of direct service to a clientele. The activities of an area council, on the other hand, consist of coordination, planning, and promotion. The councils are essentially intergroup in character.

An example of the settlement's role in neighborhood organization may be found in the activities of Union Settlement in New York City. The settlement participated in the East Harlem Council for Community Planning which was composed of citizens living in the area and professional workers—teachers, librarians, social workers, public officials. The Council was organized in 1921 and was one of the regional councils affiliated with the Welfare Council of New York City.[20] Union Settlement also sponsored a block organization scheme, carried on by the "Neighborhood Center for Block Organization," which had a store-front office with meeting rooms, in the area being organized. This scheme began in October, 1945, as a settlement extension project in block organization on an experimental basis under the direction of Dr. Rudolph M. Wittenberg. It was being conducted in an area of 20 blocks adjacent to the settlement. Each "block" consisted of the two sides of a street facing each other one block in length. The population of each ran from 800 to 1,200 people. It was a low-income interracial area of more than 26,000 people, of Italian, American Negro, Puerto Rican, and Irish backgrounds.[21] The purpose of the experiment was to determine the extent to which people in a deprived area could be enabled to grow individually as well as in groups, by taking responsibility together to effect changes in their environment.[22] Although it was started as an extension project of Union Settlement it was intended to become a total community effort on the part of all agencies, schools, churches, and other organizations. To this end the sponsorship of the East Harlem Council for Community Planning was secured.

The Neighborhood Center for Block Organization was essentially a program of direct service to individuals. It provided opportunities for, and help in, certain kinds of group experiences. Through these experiences, individuals were enabled more fully to realize many of their capacities. This was undoubtedly helpful in making possible the development of block organizations which might in turn participate as

[20] *East Harlem Council for Community Planning*, New York: East Harlem Council for Community Planning, 1947, 2 pp.

[21] Murray, Clyde E., "Successful Techniques in Social Action on a Local Level," *Proceedings of the National Conference of Social Work, 1947*, New York: Columbia University Press, 1947, p. 6.

[22] *Ibid.*, p. 7.

organizations in the community council. Although the project was involved in a community organization process, which brought many groups and agencies together, its own focus was on a group work process, bringing individuals together.

3. *Settlements Related to Community Welfare Councils*

An opportunity for discussing the relative roles of the settlement and the community council was provided by a conference called for this purpose in December, 1947.[23] A tentative definition of terms was worked out in which it was agreed to distinguish between neighborhood and district. Neighborhood was defined as "the area in which needs of preadolescent children can be met (generally speaking, the area served by the elementary school)." District was defined as "the area within a metropolitan community in which the functional needs of a major part of the population are met and in which voluntary group associations take place." [24] It is usually made up of a cluster of neighborhoods and is differentiated from all other districts by physical, psychological, and political characteristics.

It was agreed that initiating work with groups and organizations, and the developing of leadership toward the formation of a district council may be done appropriately by a settlement or any other agency seeing the need for it. Such steps, it was agreed, should be discussed with staff of the overall community welfare council who should be kept informed of developments. If the community welfare council is willing to accept responsibility, continuing sponsorship and staff service to a district council should not be given by one of its constituent members. The staffing of district councils is pri-

[23] Cleveland Conference on District and Neighborhood Community Organization, December 7-8, 1947, sponsored by Community Chests and Councils, Inc. and the National Federation of Settlements.

[24] *Report of Cleveland Conference on District and Neighborhood Community Organization, December 7-8, 1947,* New York: Community Chests and Councils, Inc., 1947, p. 3.

marily the responsibility of community welfare councils. Among problems for further study is the determination of the difference between work with groups and work with councils (intergroups). Criteria are needed for determining when community welfare council staff should be assigned to district councils and groups and to neighborhood councils and groups. Further study is also needed to determine such criteria for settlements.

E. Toward Community Welfare

1. *Area Projects*

As described in the previous chapter, a number of neighborhood area projects that started out to combat juvenile delinquency have broadened the scope of their interest to include general community betterment. These projects have been sponsored by both voluntary and public agencies. They have usually developed some form of direct service to their neighborhoods, such as case-finding, referrals, help to probationers, and recreation programs. Area projects have often encountered problems of duplicating the functions of existing agencies and have needed to relate their efforts to the central planning body concerned with health, welfare, and recreational activities of the entire community.

The Chicago Area Projects to prevent delinquency, it will be recalled, sought to develop among the residents of an area civic activities which would result in new attitudes and standards of behavior. The projects sought to help many of the people who resisted the help of social agencies. By 1947 the Russell Square and Hull House neighborhood projects had been operating for about 15 years. According to Shaw, indigenous leadership had been found. This, he believed, was significant because people in the neighborhood can make a greater contribution to the solution of problems than can an outsider. Experts had been called in to assist with projects but always, it was said, in keeping with the desires of the people. Agencies were encouraged to make staff appointments from among the residents of the neighborhood. Shaw believed that a decline in the delinquency rate was indicated by fewer arrests and the feeling of delinquents that they could come back and find their places in the community.

After speaking at a meeting of staff members of community welfare councils Shaw was challenged for minimizing the role of the professional worker, the existing agencies, and the central planning body. He was questioned regarding the make-up of his advisory board which was stated to be not representative of the group served and as having many of those characteristics of paternalism to which he objected. It was noted that the Area Projects were members of the Recreation and Education Division of the Council of Social Agencies and that they received some funds from the Community Chest.[25]

The philosophy of Shaw's Area Project was studied for application in other cities. The Baltimore Youth Commission, appointed in 1943 as an outgrowth of public concern over juvenile delinquency, sought to apply it in Baltimore. The subcommittee on "Area Projects," under the chairmanship of the Director of the Department of Public Welfare, authorized two projects in April 1944 and provided $10,000 per year for each. One was to be in an area inhabited by whites and the other in an area inhabited by Negroes. It was an experiment to arouse the inhabitants of a small section of the city to their own problems and to the responsibilities growing out of them. Each section was believed to contain sufficient potential leadership to deal effectively with its problems. It was assumed that this leadership could bring about the necessary changes, ideals, and attitudes for construction

[25] Shaw, Clifford R., "Preventing Juvenile Delinquency through Neighborhood Organization," address at Annual Meeting of Community Chests and Councils, Inc., 1947, St. Louis, joint session of Group Work Secretaries and Community Council Secretaries, pp. 2-3.

of a more acceptable community life and that reduction of delinquency depended in part on the extent to which the people themselves understood, wanted, and worked for a program of community betterment.

In addition to the director each of the areas had a full-time police officer in plain clothes to whom children in trouble were referred. The East Side Community Committee in the Negro area held huge meetings and worked through ten subcommittees with over 150 individuals serving on them. Over a period of about two years the Juvenile Protective Officer had 366 individual children assigned to him from parents or agencies. The Eastern Community Council was organized in the white area by a nominating committee set up at a mass meeting. Its Recreation Committee organized baseball leagues and other activities. By 1945 the police officer had over 100 children referred to him. After two years of operation of these projects it was believed that apathy was breaking down, unmet needs were being recognized, and there was a desire on the part of the inhabitants to do something about these needs through community organization.[26] Three additional projects were set up during the first half of 1948.

A recent study of the Baltimore projects[27] pointed out that they have tended to minimize the planning function and engage in direct service. The report stressed the need to separate the planning and direct-service functions. It was recommended that the area projects become area councils concerned with the needs of the whole community under the auspices of a public commission separate from any public agency offering a direct-service program. The report emphasized the need for close relationships with agencies offering services in the fields of health, welfare, and recreation. It

[26] Waxter, Thomas J. S., "Baltimore's Area Projects," *Public Welfare*, LV, October, 1946, pp. 233-236.

[27] Sieder, Violet M., *Study of Area Projects of the Baltimore Youth Commission*, New York: Community Chests and Councils of America, Inc., March, 1949.

proposed that the area councils be related to one another through a formal federation or association made up of delegates from the councils. Such a federation should be related formally to the Council of Social Agencies, the Commission on City Plan, and the Housing Authority. It was recommended that the Bureau of Recreation set up a new classification of recreation workers-at-large in a separate division of the Bureau to work with gangs and unorganized groups to help them to use the facilities of the established agencies. Similar work which had been done by the area coordinators was to be transferred to the Bureau.

In this way separate auspices would be provided for direct services to individuals and for coordinating the activities of agencies and organizations concerned with the needs and services of the areas. Here again are discovered the negative effects on direct service and on coordinating and planning when the two are attempted under the same auspices.

2. *Area Councils*

Area councils, as distinguished from area projects which have tended to set up organizations of individual citizens, have sought to function as interorganizational bodies, bringing together representatives of many organizations in a defined geographic area. Although some started with the limited purpose of preventing juvenile delinquency they have tended to broaden out to all problems of community welfare. They have often run the danger of developing programs of direct service and have been seen to need close working relationships with over-all community welfare councils.

The coordinating council movement which originated in California in 1919, and which was discussed in a previous chapter, grew to such an extent that by 1947 there were more than 300 coordinating councils in California and only 18 councils of social agencies.

An evaluation (mentioned in Chapter IV) of the coordinating councils of Los Angeles County which were organized in 1932, noted that by 1941 an awareness of the delinquency problem had been created in each community, recreation facilities had been developed and increased, lay participation had aroused a community sense of social responsibility, and a coordination of agencies had been achieved. In some communities the coordination achieved was of a superficial nature. In fact, there were a few councils whose scope was still narrowed by a primary concern with delinquency, and there was too much faith that delinquency could be solved by providing adequate recreation facilities. On the other hand, it was pointed out that council progress had been hampered by the lack of trained workers; that the quality of work done by some councils was impaired by "poor leadership, inadequate representation, lack of a planned program, and vague definition of purpose." One of the recommendations was that the county organization should have a staff of six or seven professional workers "trained specifically in social administration and community organization," and that the Los Angeles County Coordinating Councils be set up as an independent department. It was urged that each council conduct a campaign to increase lay participation, that the narrow aim of juvenile delinquency prevention be abandoned, and that each council take on the broader aim of community betterment, going beyond mere coordination and clearinghouse activities to become more of a "community council." [28]

It was out of motivation similar to that which gave rise to coordinating councils in California that Kansas City, Missouri, organized area councils in 1943. The Community Service Division of the Welfare Department was created by ordinance "to co-ordinate the resources of the community; to

[28] Bradley, Esther R., "An Evaluation of the Los Angeles County Coordinating Councils," *Community Coordination,* July-August, 1941, pp. 10-11.

report on social conditions; to plan and recommend programs needed to meet social problems." [29] A staff of 12 coordinators was developed. The councils covered the nine high school districts of the city and met for the most part in public schools. Membership in the area councils included representation from churches, schools, social agencies, improvement or taxpayers' associations, and individual citizens. None of the councils set up programs or operated them. Although the initial interest was youth, it was broadened to include all the affairs of the community—better recreation facilities, better street lighting, relocation of elementary school boundaries, expansion of public health services, food control, and cleanup. Being autonomous the community councils have often spoken out for civic improvements and legislation on matters affecting the lives of citizens.

The experience of Kansas City and other communities has indicated the need for close relationship between coordination and planning on the neighborhood level and that done by city planning commissions and community welfare councils on the city-wide level.

The initial purpose of the Back-of-the-Yards Neighborhood Council, organized in 1939 in the area south and west of the Chicago Stockyards, was to deal with the problem of juvenile delinquency by tackling the fundamental social problems of the area. The Council started out as an interorganizational body with planning and coordinating functions. In the course of its development its activity became concentrated upon direct service programs rather than upon coordinating and planning activities.

The immediate impetus to its organization was a study of juvenile delinquency by Saul D. Alinsky and Joseph B. Meegan. Alinsky was at that time working with Clifford Shaw as a member of the staff of the Institute for Juvenile

---

[29] *Community Service Division,* Kansas City, Missouri: Department of Welfare, July 12, 1946, p. 1.

Research. One of the conclusions of the study was that the problem of juvenile delinquency could be dealt with only by tackling the fundamental problems of living and working conditions in the area. With the support of Bishop Sheil, Alinsky and Meegan began to develop a neighborhood council of the local institutions and organizations of the people. The packing house workers' union was an important organization in the area. Bringing labor and church groups together was the starting point in the organization of the Back-of-the-Yards Neighborhood Council.

By December 31, 1948, there were 190 member organizations including churches, fraternal orders, nationality societies, athletic clubs, unions, business groups, schools, etc. A Community Congress, made up of two delegates of each member organization, considers the problems of the area and sets the emphasis in the program of the organization. The Board of Directors, consisting of one delegate from each member organization, administers the affairs of the Council. During 1948, seven Board meetings were recorded with an attendance of 75 to 80 persons.

Alinsky believed that the Council as a "People's Organization" could tackle the controversial issues that arise in dealing with the basic factors in social disorganization. He contended that the conventional community council has neither the interest nor the ability to deal with these matters. The people must develop organizations through which to generate power, to be used to fulfill a program. One of his basic premises was that a "People's Organization" could be built only by the people themselves and that they can express themselves only through *their* leaders. He contended that community councils in the past had largely coordinated only the formal agencies and had played only a superficial role in the life of the community. He assumed that if the leaders of community agencies could get to know the leaders of other community organizations, their personal opinions and attitudes would change and consequently the attitudes and policies of their respective organizations would change too.[30]

An effort to examine the significance for community organization of the Back-of-the-Yards Neighborhood Council was made in 1944 by a committee of the Recreation and Education Division of the Chicago Council of Social Agencies. The Committee stated that the Back-of-the-Yards Neighborhood Council, being inclusive of the varied interests of the community and functioning at the "grass-roots" level, was in line with developments in community organization thinking and was not something entirely new. The organization was distinctive in that it recognized a broad base of power in an industrial community as potentially providing a basis for democratic action, and also in its conception of a close relationship between local and larger-scale action. The organization's criticism of efforts to get local communities to lift themselves by their own bootstraps seemed to the Committee to be well founded. The theoretical reliance on local lay leadership, while minimizing the role of professional people, in solving problems was questioned in view of the obviously significant role played by Alinsky.[31]

In a report of an interview published in June 1947, Alinsky was quoted as expressing a desire for understanding by professional social workers since his own experience had brought modification to many of his policies and methods. He stated that appeals to chauvinism and isolationism are dangerous and should not be used as a tool in local organization; well-trained staff are needed as community organizers; the activities of a neighborhood council must be related to

[30] Alinsky, Saul D., *Reveille for Radicals*, Chicago: University of Chicago Press, 1945, p. 110.

[31] *General Principles of Community Organization and a Statement on the Back-of-the-Yards Neighborhood Council*, by a Committee of the Division on Education and Recreation, Council of Social Agencies, Chicago, April, 1944, pp. 8-9.

the efforts of social agencies and professional social workers in the area; and local neighborhood efforts should be related to over-all city-wide planning through a community welfare council. He expressed respect for the special knowledge and skill of professional social workers, and expressed his desire to work with them if they would place major emphasis on the fundamental underlying causes of poverty and social breakdown and would work to improve economic conditions, a major factor in social problems.[32]

In a recent study of the Back-of-the-Yards Neighborhood Council [33] it was observed that its activities differed from those of most councils in that direct service formed a major part of its work. The Council, in planning to meet community needs, tended to provide service itself, rather than to get one of the organizational members to offer the service, or to set up a separate body as auspice for the service. The report recommended that the Council pursue its planning function more vigorously than heretofore by a program of correlation and planning of activities among agencies and organizations within the area.

F. Community Welfare Councils

1. *Metropolis and Neighborhood*

The council of social agencies, or community welfare council, is said to provide a vehicle for a planning process aimed at bringing about a more effective adjustment between social welfare needs and resources. In this process representatives (both volunteer and professional) of operating social service units, together with representatives of other important community interests and points of view, arrive at conclusions by the conference and study method. As a result, action is taken to eliminate duplication of effort and inefficient use of funds,

[32] Sieder, Violet M., "The Council Hopper," *Community*, June, 1947, p. 207.
[33] Keeler, Howard, *Back-of-the-Yards Neighborhood Council*, Chicago: Council of Social Agencies, February, 1949.

to promote services to meet unmet needs, and to stimulate remedial and preventive measures. Certain common services may be operated by the council, such as a social service exchange and a volunteer bureau. Special studies concerning the social services may be conducted. Improvement in the quality of services may be sought. The council represents the field of health and welfare in broader activities.[34]

In 1947, there was some kind of permanent city-wide planning body for health, welfare, and recreational activities functioning in approximately 350 cities in the United States. This included all cities over 500,000 and a large proportion of those over 100,000.[35]

In this period an increasing number of councils came to recognize that the neighborhood approach was valuable in various aspects of their work and provided staff and funds for the development of community councils. In an endeavor to get at some of these problems Community Chests and Councils, Inc. sent out a questionnaire in January 1946 to the 350 member community welfare councils. The questionnaire had the limited purpose of discovering some of the developments in neighborhood organization and how widespread they were.

Out of 109 replies received, 59 said there were no community or neighborhood councils in the area covered by their over-all welfare council; 29 of this number expressed interest in neighborhood councils.

In 50 cities there were said to be neighborhood or community council developments. In 38 of these cities there were neighborhood councils affiliated with the over-all welfare council, 32 of which gave staff service and six did not. That is, in 32 cases the neighborhood councils received staff service from and were affiliated with the welfare council.

There were "joint projects" of some kind in 29 over-all

---

[34] Ford, Lyman S., "Councils in Social Work," *Social Work Year Book, 1945*, New York: Russell Sage Foundation, 1945, pp. 113-114.

[35] *Ibid.*, p. 112.

welfare councils. These were usually cooperative recreation projects involving two or more agencies. It would be interesting to know the extent to which such joint projects followed from the staff service of the secretary of the group work division. It is often this staff member of the over-all council who gives staff service when attention is first given to neighborhood councils.

In the 32 cities where neighborhood councils were affiliated to the over-all council and received staff service from it, this affiliation was often quite loose, being maintained by a staff person, or through the membership of a lay person in both councils. In some cases the neighborhood councils were officially represented in over-all councils being affiliated as member agencies, through a division or bureau of neighborhood councils. The staff service varied from advice to responsibility for helping the neighborhood councils. This was carried by the executive of the over-all council, the secretary of the group work division, or the secretary of a special bureau or department of neighborhood councils.

Twenty of these 32 over-all councils had full-time staff devoted exclusively to neighborhood councils and about 12 had staff providing part-time service. About 12 of the 32 over-all councils had special committees or neighborhood council divisions. Although these are small numbers from which to make any generalizations, they do represent significant developments.

Local community councils in the many small communities of a large metropolitan area, both within the central city and outside of it, provide one means whereby a metropolitan community welfare council may cover its total area.

2. *Some Neighborhood Council Developments*

A brief outline of what has happened in some of the larger cities will illustrate the developments reported above. These are only a few of the many cities that could be cited.

In the comprehensive reorganization of the Welfare Council of New York City in 1944 there was created a Committee on Geographic Distribution of Health and Welfare Services. The Committee sought to coordinate services at the neighborhood level. By 1946 there were 11 affiliated councils covering Brooklyn, the Bronx, Queens, and Richmond and, in fact, all but two neighborhoods in Manhattan. Staff was selected and financed jointly by the affiliated council and the Welfare Council. Many of the local councils arose on local initiative and retained a large measure of autonomy. Program and policy were determined by the local council, which maintained close liaison with the city-wide activities of the Welfare Council through staff meetings of field secretaries and regular reporting to the secretary of the Committee on Geographical Distribution. Several times a year the chairmen of regional councils met to discuss common problems and to exchange experiences. All regional councils served as information centers on the social services in their areas, sponsored open meetings of public interest, reported to the Welfare Council on gaps in welfare resources needing the help of the over-all council, and helped to further the city-wide objectives of the Welfare Council for their own constituencies.

Thus, through regional and neighborhood councils, the Welfare Council of New York City hoped to carry out its purposes more effectively. Because this form of organization was found to be effective in this regard it was continued as the permanent form of organization of the Welfare Council.

The Chicago Council of Social Agencies reported the existence of 20 active community councils in Chicago by the end of 1946. Eleven of these had been formed in the two previous years. Although the professional staff members of social agencies participated in all new councils there were only three that consisted predominantly of social agency representatives. The councils were primarily representative of churches, clubs, schools, and civic organizations. The experience of working together in Civilian Defense programs stimulated organizations to continue working together in community councils. Two of the councils were outgrowths of Civilian Defense block organizations. The Area Welfare Planning Project of the Council of Social Agencies gave advisory service to many of the councils. When local councils requested an opportunity to exchange experiences and ideas on activities and methods of organization, the Planning Project sponsored a series of informal meetings early in 1946. By the end of the year they were considering ways for joint work on problems common to all their communities.

Chicago was moving toward a closer relationship among community councils and between the local community councils and the community welfare council.

The Welfare Federation of Cleveland became interested in community councils as a result of experience with its Tremont Area Study. Intensive social study indicated that services could be made more effective if they could be more closely coordinated and if leadership of the area understood the services and promoted use of them. Citizen participation in the study of unmet needs and in action to meet them led to greater local responsibility. The original concern was juvenile delinquency. A program of prevention was developed at various levels. A case-finding service was set up which later undertook direct service to some individual children in addition to its original function of referral. It was felt that the people in the community are the ones most concerned with the services or lack of them and that they should have a greater share in the social planning job. Participation of professionals was restricted so that they would not dominate the local citizen group. Separate councils of professional workers and lay people were formed. The Central Areas and Glenville Community Councils developed. The Hough Area Council, the Kinsmen's Citizens' League, and the West Side

Community Council were developed by the Group Work
Council in the process of extending group work and recreation services. Later, steps were taken to develop citizen support and broaden the scope of these projects to cover any or
all neighborhood needs, as well as to integrate the field workers into the staff of the Federation in the same manner as
the other field workers. The councils were to provide an
opportunity for citizen thinking in local and city-wide planning. In August of 1947 the Welfare Federation of Cleveland
had 15 community councils affiliated with its Committee on
Area Councils.

Out of its rich experience in planning with neighborhood
people for needed services the Welfare Federation of Cleveland clarified the need for separate auspices for direct service
and coordinating functions. Cleveland moved toward interorganizational community councils appropriately related to
the city-wide functional councils of the Welfare Federation
and receiving community organization staff service from the
Welfare Federation of Cleveland as the over-all community
welfare council.

In Pittsburgh the impact of the war tended to wipe out
the community councils that had not been particularly active.
Whereas before the war there were 11 councils, by the mid-
dle of 1943 there were only five. The new program emphasis
was intercultural, reflecting the drive for national unity during the war. The councils helped mobilize volunteers, inter-
pret government measures, recruit blood donors, stimulate
the organization of teen-age canteens and more adequate
recreation for youth. Although two of the councils developed
direct services, the conception of community councils as
coordinating and integrating bodies, rather than as direct-
service organizations, was gaining headway. Through the
Bureau of Community Councils the Federation of Social
Agencies assumed responsibility for giving staff service to
council groups, not merely within the limits of the city of

Pittsburgh, but throughout the county. Upon the extension of staff service to communities an advisory committee to the Bureau was set up by the Association of Community Councils, in collaboration with the Federation of Social Agencies, to function as a policy-making group and to advise on the over-all program of the community councils. This body was replaced in June 1945 by the Executive Committee of the Association of Community Councils. It was to integrate the work of the community councils more closely with the other divisions of the Federation and the city-wide agencies. The Federation of Social Agencies, concerned with over-all coordination and planning, was interested in providing staff service and developing formal structural relations with these various agencies and divisions because clients and supporters could be informed more easily of services which would stimulate their increased use and support. Staff service was considered as consultative and enabling; it was not its function to direct the councils.

Through its Bureau of Community Councils, the Health and Welfare Federation of Allegheny County, as it is now called, has been developing a pattern of autonomous community councils associated with one another and related to the over-all community welfare council, the Federation. Community councils are conceived as interorganizational bodies in which are represented agencies, organizations, and groups interested in the welfare of a given community. Through the Association of Community Councils committees have been set up to study and act upon such problems of the local communities as health and education. Efforts have been made to develop close working relationships between the functional divisions of the Federation and the community councils.

Out of advisory committees established by the Los Angeles War Chest in outlying areas and the need to extend services to the new areas, district welfare councils were set up by the Welfare Federation of Los Angeles. By 1947 there were seven district welfare centers administered by the Welfare Council and financed by the Chest. It was hoped that these centers would help solve some of the difficulties faced by agencies attempting to serve distant and unfamiliar neighborhoods. Also, the Welfare Council of Metropolitan Los Angeles wanted to broaden the base of citizen participation in social welfare planning. Each welfare center housed from ten to twelve Chest-financed services, and some were used by public agencies. Each center was independent and autonomous as to membership, bylaws, and program. In order to relate the district welfare councils to the over-all Welfare Council and to the coordinating councils already operating in the same area, the Welfare Council organized a Department of District Planning. This department had an advisory committee, which included two members from each district council, and which coordinated the programs of the district councils. The chairman was a member of the Executive Board of the Welfare Council.

The Los Angeles developments present a perspective of operating agencies cooperating at the local district level together with citizen organizations in autonomous welfare centers, which are in turn related to the metropolitan community welfare council.

These examples of the integration of neighborhood organization with community-wide organization for social welfare represent a trend which is the outgrowth of efforts we have noted in our examination of previous periods. Some of these efforts at neighborhood organization were concerned with organization from within the neighborhoods while others approached neighborhoods from the outside. Community councils on a neighborhood or district basis constitute a significant means of integrating these approaches with community-wide organization for social welfare.

CONCLUSION: A FORWARD LOOK

1. *Neighborhood Organization Functions*

The background of neighborhood organization since the Civil War shows that many of our fundamental social problems have persisted since the industrial revolution. As suggested at the outset of this study neighborhood organization alone will not change the social conditions from which our fundamental social problems arise and in which they thrive. The remedies for such conditions as low incomes, unemployment, and substandard housing must be as basic as the causes and, therefore, must go beyond the scope of neighborhood organization for social welfare. However, people need opportunities to do something in their neighborhoods about these conditions. Further, society has provided a number of health and welfare services to help those affected adversely. These services, offered through a multitude of governmental and voluntary agencies, are not always available in neighborhoods and districts in a coordinated way. In attempts to deal with these problems a variety of forms of neighborhood organization have been devised and have been used with varying degrees of success. We have noted some of the principles by which they have succeeded and some of the reasons

157

for failure. What does all this tell us about what we should do in neighborhood organization today?

Vigorous efforts are needed today in neighborhood organization to make services available, to offer integrated patterns of services to meet the varying needs of neighborhoods and districts, to coordinate services to prevent overlapping and overlooking, to provide opportunities at the neighborhood and district levels for people to form groups through which they can act together, and to provide channels for groups to act together to change social goals and create new ones. In carrying out these functions the keynote must be the participation in these processes of people in their neighborhoods —where families live, shop, go to school and church, and where they vote.

Health and welfare agencies have developed specialized functions and have tended to operate out of central offices with consequent disadvantages as well as advantages. Quite often this has cut off valuable close contact with the organizations and agencies within the neighborhoods and districts of the area served. It is because of gaps in the channels of communication to and from the neighborhoods that health and welfare agencies are often bypassed by churches, parent-teacher associations, and other neighborhood groups which set up direct-service projects under their own sponsorship. Centrally administered direct-service agencies can help to prevent this by making their services available to people in neighborhoods on a decentralized basis. District advisory committees can provide a channel through which the neighborhood supporters and users of the services can participate in policy-making and help to make the services available. These committees can be represented by delegates on the district community council.

We have lost some of the values inherent in the integration of services in neighborhoods and districts which were realized by the charity organization societies and the settlements.

These values might be regained today through the development of the potential of settlements and community centers to make available a variety of services, under many auspices, in one place in the neighborhood or district.

In addition to making available a variety of health and welfare services the settlement can develop recognition of a need, set up a new service on a demonstration basis, and then seek permanent auspices for it. This function has brought into existence many of our basic health, welfare, and recreational services. Another major contribution of the settlement is to help people to form groups through which they can act together and say what they think is needed for the welfare of the community. Such groups as neighborhood associations can play a significant role as constituent groups in a district community council. The settlements can help those interested in the formation of a district community council to take their initial steps and can itself participate as a member agency.

As we look back at the conception of the school as the place for all to become acquainted, to discuss, and to organize for civic improvement, the polling place, the center for employment, recreation, health, and culture, it appears as reasonable and desirable today as it did when it was conceived. But the school has not become this kind of agency, and, like the settlement, it has not brought about the degree of integration of services needed. However, this concept of the school has influenced developments. In many cities the use of school buildings for recreational activities, adult education programs, and health clinics, in addition to the formal education of children, has become quite extensive. Increasing recognition of the conditions and agencies which are important to the school's effectiveness has been bringing school teachers and administrators into participation in community affairs in neighborhoods and districts. As educators succeed in gaining acceptance for more comprehensive concepts of education the broader potentials of the school will be realized.

It took a great deal of experimenting on the part of councils of social agencies and later community welfare councils before it became clear that district community councils represent a significant and, in many cases, a necessary form of organization through which their work might be made more effective. Community welfare councils, as centralized coordinating and planning bodies which coordinate the activities of a large number of voluntary and tax-supported health and welfare services, need district community councils to facilitate citizen participation in action to change social conditions and to make available in neighborhoods and districts the services of city-wide agencies.

The district community council, as a coordinating, interorganizational body related functionally to the community welfare council, is a means through which the direct-service agencies in health, welfare, recreation and education, and citizen organizations may work together within the larger context of the city or metropolitan area as a whole. The cooperative effort of citizen organizations and social agencies on problems in neighborhoods can be the beginning of work which may be extended to as broad an area as a solution may require. The district community council can help to meet today's need for neighborhood organization, not only by virtue of its own activities as an interorganizational body, but also by the activities it can stimulate in direct-service agencies and citizen groups. Because of this, the district community council has a key place in neighborhood organization today.

2. *The District Community Council*

Some of the unique functions of a district community council, as set forth by professional staff workers from a number of cities,[1] are as follow: (1) Coordination of health and welfare services at the neighborhood level; (2) helping people to become articulate about their needs and enlisting their participation in meeting them; (3) serving as a medium for the interchange of ideas among rank and file professionals; (4) serving as a medium for joint planning and action by agencies and civic groups; (5) providing a means for communicating to the city-wide level the neighborhood view of problems.

When it is seen in this light, neighborhood organization is of value, not only for "problem areas," but for all areas served by a community welfare council—urban, suburban, and semi-urban. It offers to councils of social agencies another way of broadening into councils that are not only concerned with, but are representative of the welfare of the whole community. It is neither possible nor advisable for a city-wide council to attempt to impose an elaborate scheme of neighborhood organization upon a metropolitan area. It is possible—perhaps even advisable—to have a considered policy for developing neighborhood or district councils, because they can strengthen the work of a community welfare council.

Neighborhood and district organization may prove to be a significant approach to the community organization problems of metropolitan areas. Such areas are made up of numerous separate communities in many of which there is an intense feeling of local pride. Although to democratic institutions this is often a source of great strength, in community organization it has made difficult the development of a

---

[1] "Minutes of meeting of neighborhood council secretaries of community welfare councils at the National Conference of Social Work," August 5, 1946. There was expressed at this meeting a need for study of neighborhood councils to develop a body of knowledge and experience about them. (From mimeographed copy in the files of Community Chests and Councils, Inc., New York.)

large enough unit to warrant the specialized staff that is needed today. A metropolitan council in which the constituent communities have their own district councils may make it possible for smaller communities to do their own planning within the larger framework and to have available the specialized staff and committees of the functional divisions of the over-all council.

In a district community council it is possible to bring together the representatives of the various agencies and organizations that exist in a district. It is often possible to get participation of groups and organizations that are rarely reached at the city-wide level. Furthermore, it is the lower echelons of leadership that are reached in the agencies and organizations. These are the leaders who work directly with the people of the community, for example, the local librarian, the leader of the parent-teacher association, the school principal, the trade union official, the parish priest, local ministers, the president of the fraternal order, the case worker, the group worker, the playground supervisor, and the district nurse, among others.

The distinction between neighborhood and district which was made some time ago by settlement people is deserving of wider acceptance. A neighborhood is roughly the area served by an elementary school. It may be an eighth to a half mile in extent. A district, however, includes several elementary school areas and is roughly the area served by a high school. The so-called "neighborhood council" is often not an interorganizational body because the neighborhood is too small an area in which to find enough organized groups. Local interorganizational councils need the larger area of a district in which there exists a sufficient number and variety of organized groups.

Enthusiasm for a neighborhood project often carries the district council into the sponsorship of direct services. But if it develops such a program it will get into conflict with the agencies whose function it is to offer services. A district community council can be more effective if its efforts are focused upon getting appropriate agencies to assume these responsibilities. Moving into the direct-service field also keeps the council from doing its real work of bringing groups together to study the needs of the district and to work out plans by which the direct-service agencies might meet them. Similarly, a direct-service agency, such as a settlement, a youth serving agency, or a family agency, gets into difficulty when it attempts to bring together other direct-service agencies, as our study has shown.

In bringing together the various organized groups in the district the council should be instrumental in stimulating discussion within the constituent groups. To do this effectively, the council should be composed primarily of delegates of the organizations of the district. The thinking of the community can be more adequately expressed by representatives of organized groups than by selected individuals who are "leading citizens." Often the effectiveness of the latter stems from their conscious or unconscious representation of groups. It is hazardous for a district council to reflect the personal sentiments of certain individuals rather than those of the organizations of the community.

Workers in the field have expressed the conviction that the professional staff of district councils should concentrate on helping neighborhood groups in their relations with other groups and with the agencies of the community. Delegates of local groups should be helped to report back to their groups on the matters discussed and on the decisions made in local council meetings. In this way the community will participate in determining its needs and in taking action through the district council. Skill is needed in helping delegates work out differences amid tensions. Staff people are needed who have the knowledge and skill to help a great diversity of groups see their common interests and work together on them. A positive appreciation of ethnic, racial, religious, and other differences is important. The breadth of representation that district councils can potentially attain may help overcome the social barriers that have excluded significant groupings from community planning activities.

The profession of social work is beginning to make a contribution to analysis of the process of community organization.[2] Professional social workers are needed who understand these processes and who can give professional service to those involved in them. Much work remains to be done in clarifying the nature of social work practice in community organization.[3]

Neighborhood councils need a degree of autonomy in keeping with their local character. They need complete independence in matters of a purely local nature and an appropriate part in making decisions that affect other neighborhoods in addition to their own.

In a progress report on a nationwide study of community councils given in December 1948,[4] Violet M. Sieder stated that in neighborhood and district councils there was an increasing emphasis upon citizen participation in social planning, rather than upon the operation of services. The make-up of councils tended to shift from membership of individuals to membership of organizations. The formation of an association of community councils seemed to help them to function more effectively. The councils were covering larger areas consisting of several neighborhoods. Many experiments were being conducted with channels to the divi-

---

[2] Newstetter, Wilber I., "The Social Intergroup Work Process: How Does It Differ from the Social Group Work Process?" in Howard, Donald S., ed., *Community Organization, Its Nature and Setting*, New York: American Association of Social Workers, American Association for the Study of Community Organization, Community Chests and Councils, Inc., 1947.

[3] Dillick, Sidney, "Some Problems of Social Work Practice in Community Organization," *Proceedings of the Fourth Biennial Alumni-Faculty Conference, School of Social Work, University of Pittsburgh, April, 1949*, p. 141.

[4] In the files of Community Chests and Councils of America, New York.

sions and departments of the central welfare council. Staff service to local units was recognized as necessary if the district councils were to function as part of community planning machinery. The staff was most successful when it had professional training and experience. Part of its responsibility was to call on experts from housing authorities, city planning organizations, interracial commissions, and the specialized staffs of community welfare councils as consultants to work with local councils on specific community problems. The successful results of participation of local civic associations in district councils pointed to the need for over-all councils to find ways in which metropolitan civic and citizen organizations could participate in their activities.

Many questions remain to be answered. The report pointed out that there is need to distinguish between the function of a district council and the functions of neighborhood groups organized by settlements, Urban Leagues, schools, etc. Exploration is needed of the extent to which youth councils can be successfully organized on a neighborhood basis, as a part of or separate from a city-wide youth council. There is a need for criteria for establishing priority among requests for staff service to district councils in terms of the economic and social status of the area, the readiness of the community to organize, its ability to finance staff, etc. The desirable unit for district community council staff by population and geographic size has yet to be determined. How should district councils be financed? By grants from the community chest? As part of over-all council operation? Are district offices important? Continued study is needed on the relation of district councils to over-all community welfare councils.

For a long time community welfare councils (and councils of social agencies) have been concerned with bringing together people and services. This has usually pointed in one direction only—from the agencies to the people. Through district community councils which are closely related to over-all welfare councils, not only can neighborhoods and districts obtain financial and technical resources, but they can also make the larger community aware of gaps and inequalities of service. District community councils can have their great-est effect when they are represented in divisions and depart-ments, and when they use the community welfare council staff. Through this close tie it becomes possible for the over-all council to maintain sensitivity to the needs of the people and to enlist the participation of neighborhoods in getting needs met. Through district community councils in a metro-politan area neighborhood groups can participate in activity which furthers the well-being of the neighborhood and of the larger community.

Throughout this study we have seen how neighborhood organization takes form in social welfare activities. In every period we have seen that it has had a significant place. The neighborhood and district levels of organization have their places among city, county, state, national, and international levels. In fact, neighborhood organization makes a unique contribution to social welfare, since efforts to solve the prob-lems of social well-being are ultimately tested in their ability to meet the common human needs of individuals and families in their neighborhoods.

BIBLIOGRAPHY

Addams, Jane. "The Chicago Settlements and Social Unrest," *Charities and Commons*, XX, May, 1908.

Addams, Jane. "A Function of the Social Settlement," *Annals of the American Academy of Political and Social Science, 1899,* XIII, Philadelphia: American Academy of Political and Social Science, 1899.

Addams, Jane. *Philanthropy and Social Progress,* New York: Thomas Y. Crowell, 1893.

Addams, Jane. *Second Twenty Years at Hull House,* New York: Macmillan, 1930.

Addams, Jane. *Twenty Years at Hull House* (Rev. ed.), New York: Macmillan, 1910.

"Adult Education and Civilian Defense: Four Community Programs," *Adult Education Bulletin,* VII, February, 1943.

Alinsky, Saul D. "Community Analysis and Organization," *American Journal of Sociology,* XLVI, May, 1941.

Alinsky, Saul D. *Reveille for Radicals,* Chicago: University of Chicago Press, 1945.

Barry, Mildred C. "Co-operative Planning for Co-ordinated Neighborhood Service," *Annual Volume of the New York State Conference on Social Work,* Syracuse: New York State Conference on Social Work, 1945.

Beam, Kenneth S. "Community Coordination—National Survey," *Yearbook of the National Probation Association, 1937,* New York: National Probation Association, 1937.

Beam, Kenneth S. "Community Coordination for the Prevention of Delinquency," *Yearbook of the National Probation*

Association, 1936, New York: National Probation Association, 1936.

Beam, Kenneth S. "Community Councils in 1918 and 1941," *Community Coordination,* VIII, November-December, 1940.

Beam, Kenneth S. "Conference on Coordinating and Neighborhood Councils," *Probation,* XIV, June, 1936.

Beam, Kenneth S. "Coordinating Council Progress—National Survey," *Yearbook of the National Probation Association, 1938,* New York: National Probation Association, 1938.

Beam, Kenneth S. *Coordinating Councils in California,* Sacramento: California State Printing Office, 1938.

Bookman, C. M. "The Community Chest Movement—An Interpretation," *Proceedings of the National Conference of Social Work, 1924,* Chicago: University of Chicago Press, 1924.

Bookman, C. M. "The Relation between Neighborhood Work and Financial Federations," *Proceedings of the National Conference of Social Work, 1924,* Chicago: University of Chicago Press, 1924.

Borst, Homer W. "Community Chests and Councils," *Social Work Year Book, 1929,* New York: Russell Sage Foundation, 1929.

Bowman, Leroy E. "Between Neighbors," *Survey,* LIII, December, 1924.

Bowman, Leroy E. "Community Centers," *Social Work Year Book, 1929,* New York: Russell Sage Foundation, 1929.

Bowman, Leroy E. "Community Organization," *Social Work Year Book, 1929,* New York: Russell Sage Foundation, 1929.

Bowman, Leroy E. "Community Organization," *American Journal of Sociology,* XXXV, May, 1930.

Bowman, Leroy E. "Community Progress: Developments in Community Organization," *Social Forces,* V, September, 1926.

Bowman, Leroy E. "Development of Coordination in Neighborhood Organization in New York City," *Proceedings of the National Conference of Social Work, 1924,* Chicago: University of Chicago Press, 1924.

Bowman, Leroy E. "Group and Community Organization," *The American Journal of Sociology,* XXXIV, July, 1928.

Bowman, Leroy E. "Group and Community Organization," *The American Journal of Sociology,* XXXIV, May, 1929.

Bowman, Leroy E. "The 1929 Content of the Community Concept," *Journal of Social Forces,* VII, March, 1929.

Bowman, Leroy E. "Population Mobility and Community Organization," *American Sociological Society, Papers and Proceedings, 1926,* Chicago: American Sociological Society, 1926.

Bowman, Leroy E. "Some Difficulties in Democratic Neighborhood Organization as Illustrated in Bowling Green, New York City," *Journal of Social Forces,* III, March, 1925.

Bowman, Leroy E. "Tangible Results of Co-ordination of Health and Family Welfare Work in a Defined City Area," *Social Forces,* IV, December, 1925.

Brackett, Jeffrey R. "The Charity Organization Movement: Its Tendency and Its Duty," *Proceedings of the National Conference of Charities and Correction, 1895,* Boston: George H. Ellis, 1895.

Brackett, Jeffrey R. "District Charity Organization," *The Charities Review,* VII, September, 1897.

Brackett, Jeffrey R. *Supervision and Education in Charity,* New York: Macmillan, 1903.

Bradley, Esther R. "An Evaluation of the Los Angeles County Coordinating Councils," *Community Coordination,* IX, July-August, 1941.

Brandt, Lillian. *The Charity Organization Society of New York, 1882-1907,* New York: Charity Organization Society, 1907.

Brown, Josephine C. *Public Relief: 1929-1939,* New York: Henry Holt and Co., 1940.

Brunner, Edmund de S. "Adult Education," *Social Work Year Book, 1935,* New York: Russell Sage Foundation, 1935.

Buell, Bradley. "The Settlement and Its Foreign Born Neighbor," *Journal of Social Forces,* VII, December, 1928.

Burch, Glen. "Adult Education," *Social Work Year Book, 1947,* New York: Russell Sage Foundation, 1947.

Burch, Glen. "Evaluating Adult Education: Some Principles for a Community-Centered Program," *Adult Education Journal,* VI, April, 1947.

Burchard, Edward L. "Can We Make Emergency Coordination Permanent?" *Community Coordination,* IX, January-February, 1941.

Burgess, Ernest W. "Can Neighborhood Work Have a Scientific

Basis?" *Proceedings of the National Conference of Social Work, 1924,* Chicago: University of Chicago Press, 1924.

Burgess, Ernest W. "The Natural Area as the Unit for Social Work in the Large City," *Proceedings of the National Conference of Social Work, 1926,* Chicago: University of Chicago Press, 1926.

Burgess, Ernest W., Lohman, Joseph D., and Shaw, Clifford R. "The Chicago Area Project," *Yearbook of the National Probation Association, 1937,* New York: National Probation Association, 1937.

Burnett, Mary Clarke. "The Pittsburgh Community Council," *Midmonthly Survey,* LXVIII, May, 1932.

Campbell, W. "Community Organization in Colorado," *Adult Education Bulletin,* VII, December, 1942.

Carner, Lucy P. *Why New Settlements?* Chicago: Howell Neighborhood House, April, 1945 (Mimeographed).

Childs, Clinton S. *A Year's Experiment in Social Center Organization,* New York: People's Institute, 1913.

Coit, Stanton. *Neighborhood Guilds: An Instrument of Social Reform,* London: Swan, Sonneschein and Co., 1891.

Cole, W. I. *Motives and Results of the Social Settlement Movement,* Publications of Harvard University Department of Social Ethics, No. 2, 1908.

Colcord, Joanna C. "Relief, Style 1936," *Proceedings of the National Conference of Social Work, 1936,* Chicago: University of Chicago Press, 1936.

Collier, John. "Community Councils—Democracy Every Day I," *Survey,* XL, August 31, 1918.

Collier, John. "Community Councils—Democracy Every Day II," *Survey,* XL, September 21, 1918.

Collier, John. "Community Councils—Democracy Every Day III," *Survey,* XL, September 28, 1918.

Collier, John. "Social Centers," *National Municipal Review,* II, July, 1913.

The Community Center, New York: National Community Center Association, October-December, 1920.

The Community Council: A Natural Outgrowth of the Defense Council, Washington: U. S. Office of Civilian Defense, 1945.

Community Education in Action—A Report on Community Organization of the American Association for Adult Edu-

cation, New York: American Association for Adult Education (through the cooperation of the Institute of Adult Education, Teachers College, Columbia University), 1948.

Community Service Division, Kansas City, Missouri: Department of Welfare, July, 1946 (Mimeographed).

Crime Commission of New York State. *Crime in the Community: A Study of Trends in Crime Prevention by the Sub-Commission on Causes and Effects of Crime,* Albany: J. B. Lyon Co., 1930.

Dahir, James. *The Spread and Acceptance of the Neighborhood Unit Plan—A Bibliography,* New York: Russell Sage Foundation, 1947.

Daniels, John. *America Via the Neighborhood,* New York: Harper and Bros., 1920.

Dawson, John B. "Community Chests," *Social Work Year Book, 1947,* New York: Russell Sage Foundation, 1947.

de Forest, Robert W. "What Is Charity Organization?" *Charities,* I, November, 1891.

Deming, R. C. "Connecticut's Citizens' Councils," *Adult Education Journal,* III, April, 1944.

Devine, Edward T. "The Spirit of Charity," *Charities,* VIII, January 11, 1902.

Devine, Edward T. "The Dominant Note of Modern Philanthropy," *Proceedings of the National Conference of Charities and Correction, 1906,* Chicago: University of Chicago Press, 1906.

Devine, Edward T. "Philanthropy and Business," *Survey,* XXXII, June, 1914.

Devine, Edward T. "Pittsburgh the Year of the Survey," *The Pittsburgh Survey* (Volume on the Pittsburgh District, Civic Frontage), New York: Survey Associates, 1914.

Devine, Edward T. "The Social Unit in Cincinnati," *The Survey,* XLIII, November, 1919.

Devine, Edward T. and Assistants. "Citizens' Association of a Unique Community," *Sociology and Social Research,* XIII, November-December, 1928.

Dewey, John and Evelyn. *Schools of Tomorrow,* New York: E. P. Dutton & Co., 1915.

Dickey, Roosevelt. "Better Neighborhoods—Better People," *Community,* XXI, September, 1945.

Dillick, Sidney. "The Neighborhood Approach to Community Planning," *Canadian Welfare,* March, 1947.

Dillick, Sidney. "Some Problems of Social Work Practice in Community Organization," *Proceedings of the Fourth Biennial Alumni-Faculty Conference, School of Social Work, University of Pittsburgh, April, 1949.*

Dinwiddie, Courtenay. *Community Responsibility* (A Review of the Cincinnati Social Unit Experiment), New York: New York School of Social Work, 1922.

The District Committee, Charity Organization Society of New York, December, 1917.

Dunham, Arthur. *Community Councils in Action,* Philadelphia and Pittsburgh: Public Charities Association of Pennsylvania, 1929.

Dunham, Arthur. "The Literature of Community Organization," *Proceedings of the National Conference of Social Work, 1940,* New York: Columbia University Press, 1940.

Earle, Genevieve B. "The Meaning of the Community Center Movement," *Journal of Social Forces,* III, January, 1925.

East Harlem Council for Community Planning, New York: East Harlem Council for Community Planning, 1947 (Mimeographed).

Elderton, Marion (ed.). *Case Studies of Unemployment,* Philadelphia: University of Pennsylvania Press, 1931.

Eldridge, Seba. "Community Organization and Citizenship," *Journal of Social Forces,* VII, September, 1928.

Emergency Program for the National Citizens' Committee, Association of Community Chests and Councils, January 1–June 30, 1933. (In the files of Community Chests and Councils of America, Inc., under "Community Chests—History and Development.")

Esgar, Mildred S. "Area Projects in Cleveland," *Journal of Educational Sociology,* XVIII, March, 1945.

Extracts from a Paper Upon District Conferences (Given by Mrs. James T. Fields of Boston), New York Charity Organization Society Papers, No. 3, May, 1882.

Farra, Kathryn. "Neighborhood Councils," *Proceedings of the National Conference of Social Work, 1940,* New York: Columbia University Press, 1940.

Fifteen Years of Community Council Development: A Report Presented at the Evaluation Committee Meeting of the

Association of Community Councils of Pittsburgh and Allegheny County, Pittsburgh: Federation of Social Agencies, 1946 (Mimeographed).

Financial Federations: Report of a Special Committee, New York: American Association for Organizing Charity, 1917.

Fink, Arthur E. *The Field of Social Work,* New York: Henry Holt and Co., 1942.

"The First National Conference on Coordinating Councils," *Yearbook of the National Probation Association, 1936,* New York: National Probation Association, 1936.

Folks, Homer. "Functions of a Social Settlement," *Charities,* VIII, May, 1908.

Folks, Homer. "Fundamental Objectives of a Council of Social Agencies," *Proceedings of the National Conference of Social Work, 1928,* Chicago: University of Chicago Press, 1928.

Follett, Mary Parker. *The New State,* New York: Longmans, Green and Co., 1918.

Ford, Lyman S. "The Effect of World War II on Community Organization for Health and Welfare," *Proceedings of the National Conference of Social Work, 1944,* New York: Columbia University Press, 1944.

Ford, Lyman S. "Councils in Social Work," *Social Work Year Book, 1945,* New York: Russell Sage Foundation, 1945.

Ford, Robert S. and Miner, Francis H. *An Experiment in Community Improvement,* Bureau of Government, University of Michigan, 1942.

"The Function of the Social Settlement" (A synopsis of articles by Mary K. Simkhovitch, Homer Folks, E. J. Urwick and J. B. Reynolds), *Charities,* VIII, May, 1902.

General Principles of Community Organization and a Statement on the Back-of-the-Yards Neighborhood Council (Report of a Committee of the Division on Education and Recreation), Chicago: Council of Social Agencies, April, 1944 (Mimeographed).

Gillette, J. M. "Community Concepts," *Journal of Social Forces,* IV, June, 1926.

Gillin, J. L. "Economic Aspects of the Community that Determine the Nature and Extent of Comprehensive Democratic Organization," *Proceedings of the National Conference of Social Work, 1925,* Chicago: University of Chicago Press, 1925.

Gilman, Robbins. "Leadership Strategy in Community Organization: The Development of Local Initiative," *Proceedings of the National Conference of Social work, 1925,* Chicago: University of Chicago Press, 1925.

Glueck, Eleanor T. *Community Use of Schools,* Baltimore: Williams and Wilkins, 1927.

Goodale, F. A. (ed.). *Literature of Philanthropy,* New York: Harper and Bros., 1893.

Graham, Perle D. "The Cleveland Study of Community Centers from the Standpoint of the Schools and Private Effort," *Proceedings of the National Conference of Social Work, 1931,* Chicago: University of Chicago Press, 1931.

A Guide to Community Coordination, Los Angeles: Co-ordinating Councils, Inc., 1941.

Guild, Arthur A. "The Organization of Social Work by Neighborhoods," *Yearbook of the National Probation Association, 1936,* New York: National Probation Association, 1936.

Gurteen, S. Humphreys V. *Handbook of Charity Organization,* Buffalo: published by the author, 1882.

Hale, E. E. (ed.). Editorial, *Lend-a-Hand,* XIII, November, 1894.

Hall, John F. "The Administration and Supervision of Community Councils," *Yearbook of the National Probation Association, 1937,* New York: National Probation Association, 1937.

Hart, Helen. "The Changing Functions of the Settlement under Changing Conditions," *Proceedings of the National Conference of Social Work, 1931,* Chicago: University of Chicago Press, 1931.

Hart, Joseph K. *Community Organization,* New York: Macmillan, 1920.

Haydon, Edward. "Community Organization and Crime Prevention," *Yearbook of the National Probation Association, 1942,* New York: National Probation Association, 1942.

Health and Welfare Planning in the Smaller Community, New York: Community Chests and Councils, Inc., 1945.

Hendry, Charles E. "Lay Participation in Improving Environment," *Yearbook of the National Probation Association, 1936,* New York: National Probation Association, 1936.

History of the Community Chest, 1928, New York: Association of Community Chests and Councils, Bulletin No. 44.

Holden, A. C. *The Settlement Idea,* New York: Macmillan, 1922.

Hunt, H. C. and Leonard, J. P. "Participation in Community Co-ordination and Planning," *Forty-fifth Yearbook of the National Society for the Study of Education, 1946,* Chicago: Society for the Study of Education, 1946.

Hunter, Robert. "Social Settlements and Charity Organization," *Journal of Political Economy,* XI, December, 1902.

Inter-Council Newsletter, New York: Institute of Adult Education, Teachers College, Columbia University, April, 1944.

Jackson, Henry E. *The Community Center—What It Is and How to Organize It,* Washington: U. S. Bureau of Education, No. 11, 1918.

Johnson, Arlien. "The Obstacle of Limited Participation in Local Social Planning," *Proceedings of the National Conference of Social Work, 1940,* New York: Columbia University Press, 1940.

Kahn, Dorothy. "Community Organization for What?" *Better Times,* XXVIII, May, 1947.

Kaiser, Clara. *Study of Area Projects of the Group Work Council of the Welfare Federation of Cleveland,* Cleveland: Welfare Federation, 1945 (Mimeographed).

Keeler, Howard. *Back-of-the-Yards Neighborhood Council,* Chicago: Council of Social Agencies, February, 1949 (Mimeographed).

Kellogg, Charles D. "Charity Organization in the United States," *Proceedings of the National Conference of Charities and Correction, 1893,* Madison: Midland Publishing Co., 1893.

Kellogg, Paul U. "Our Hidden Cities and the American Zest for Discovery," *Survey Graphic,* LX, July, 1928.

Kellogg, Paul U. "Social Settlements," *Encyclopedia of the Social Sciences,* XIV, 1934.

Kennedy, Albert J. (ed.). *Settlement Goals for the Next Third of a Century,* Boston: National Federation of Settlements, 1926.

Kennedy, Albert J. "The District as a Unit for Community Organization," *Journal of Social Forces,* V, March, 1927.

Kennedy, Albert J. "Social Settlements," *Social Work Year Book, 1929,* New York: Russell Sage Foundation, 1929.

Kennedy, Albert J. "Social Settlements," *Encyclopaedia Britannica,* 14th ed., XX, 1940.

Kennedy, Isabel. "When You Budget You Plan," *Community,* XXII, October, 1946.

Klein, Philip. *A Social Study of Pittsburgh,* New York: Columbia University Press, 1938.

Krughoff, Merrill F. "Councils in Social Work," *Social Work Year Book, 1947,* New York: Russell Sage Foundation, 1947.

Lane, Robert P. "Many Neighborhoods—One City," *Community,* XXI, February, 1946.

Lindeman, Eduard C. "New Trends in Community Control," *Proceedings of the National Conference of Social Work, 1932,* Chicago: University of Chicago Press, 1932.

Luke, Robert A. "Committee on Community Organization: A Progress Report," *Adult Education Journal,* VI, April, 1947.

Luke, Robert A. "Illinois Community Cooperation," *Adult Education Journal,* III, April, 1944.

McAllister, R. and Luke, Robert A. "Chicago Block Discussion Program," *Adult Education Journal,* II, October, 1943.

McClenahan, B. A. *Organizing the Community,* New York: Century, 1922.

McClusky, Howard Y. "Some Current Trends in Community Organization," *Adult Education Bulletin,* X, February, 1946.

McCullough, W. T. "Organizing Social Services by Neighborhoods," *Community,* XV, June, 1939.

McCullough, W. T. "Progress 'Between Stacks and Spires,'" *Community,* XVII, April, 1942.

McDowell, John. *General Report of the Cleveland Settlement Study,* Cleveland: Welfare Federation, 1946.

McDowell, Mary E. "The House of Service in the Chicago Stockyards District," *Survey,* XXXI, December, 1913.

McKenzie, R. D. *The Neighborhood: A Study of Local Life in the City of Columbus, Ohio,* Chicago: University of Chicago Press, 1923.

McLean, Francis H. *The Central Council of Social Agencies,* New York: American Association for Organizing Family Social Work, 1920.

McLean, Francis H. "Central Councils and Community Planning," *Survey*, XXXVIII, June, 1917.

McLean, Francis H. *Charity Organization Field Work*, New York: Russell Sage Foundation, 1910.

McLean, Francis H. "Societies for Organizing Charity," *Survey*, XXVIII, July, 1912.

McLennan, William E. "Democracy and the Settlement," *Journal of Social Forces*, IV, June, 1926.

McMillen, A. Wayne. *Community Organization for Social Welfare*, Chicago: University of Chicago Press, 1945.

McMillen, A. Wayne. "Community Organization in Chicago— 1945," *Social Service Review*, XIX, June, 1945.

McMillen, A. Wayne. "Community Organization in Social Work," *Social Work Year Book, 1947*, New York: Russell Sage Foundation, 1947.

McMillen, A. Wayne. "The Council of Social Agencies and Community Planning," *Proceedings of the National Conference of Social Work, 1932*, Chicago: University of Chicago Press, 1932.

"The Men's Community Club," *The Commons*, VI, May, 1901.

Montgomery, J. H. "Principles of Organization in Community Councils," *Journal of Social Forces*, V, September, 1926.

Morgan, Arthur E. *The Small Community*, New York: Harper and Bros., 1942.

Murray, Clyde E. *New Horizons for the Settlement Movement*, New York: National Federation of Settlements, 1944.

Murray, Clyde E. "Successful Techniques in Social Action on a Local Level," *Proceedings of the National Conference of Social Work, 1947*, New York: Columbia University Press, 1947.

"Nashville, Tennessee, Block Plan for Defense," *Community Coordination*, IX, No. 5, September-October, 1941.

"National Organizations Assist Local Councils," *Community Coordination*, IX, January-February, 1941.

The Neighborhood Approach to Community Planning, New York: Community Chests and Councils, Inc., Bulletin No. 94, 1937.

The Neighborhood Center for Block Organization (A Statement of Function and Program), New York: Neighborhood Center for Block Organization, September, 1946 (Mimeographed).

Newstetter, Wilber I. "The Social Intergroup Work Process: How Does It Differ from the Social Group Work Process?" in Howard, Donald S., ed., *Community Organization, Its Nature and Setting,* New York: American Association of Social Workers, Association for the Study of Community Organization, Community Chests and Councils, Inc., 1947.

New York City Charity Organization Society, Twenty-fifth Annual Report, New York: 1907.

North, Cecil Clare. *The Community and Social Welfare: A Study in Community Organization,* New York: McGraw Hill, 1931.

Norton, William J. *The Co-operative Movement in Social Work,* New York: Macmillan, 1927.

Notes on Community Center Work in School Buildings, New York: Social Center Committee, People's Institute, Pamphlet No. 1, March, 1915.

Paine, Robert T., Jr. "Pauperism in Great Cities: Its Four Chief Causes," *Proceedings of the International Congress of Charities, Correction, and Philanthropy, 1893,* I, Baltimore: The Johns Hopkins Press, 1894.

Park, Robert E. "Community Organization and the Romantic Temper," *Journal of Social Forces,* III, May, 1925.

Peabody, Francis G. "The Problem of Charity," *Charities Review,* III, November, 1893.

Peck, Lillie M. *General Report on Field Work,* New York: National Federation of Settlements, April, 1920.

Perry, Clarence A. *Evening Recreation Centers,* New York: Russell Sage Foundation, 1910.

Perry, Clarence A. *Wider Use of the School Plant,* New York: Survey Associates, 1913.

Perry, Clarence A. *School Center Gazette, 1919-1920,* New York: Russell Sage Foundation, 1920.

Perry, Clarence A. "The Relation of Neighborhood Forces to the Larger Community: Planning a City Neighborhood from the Social Point of View," *Proceedings of the National Conference of Social Work, 1924,* Chicago: University of Chicago Press, 1924.

Perry, Clarence A. "Social Center History in Chicago," *Journal of Social Forces,* III, January, 1925.

Perry, Clarence A. "The Rehabilitation of the Local Community," *Journal of Social Forces,* IV, March, 1926.

Perry, Clarence A. *The Neighborhood Unit, Regional Survey of New York and Its Environs,* VII, New York: Russell Sage Foundation, 1930.

Perry, Clarence A. and Williams, Marguerita P. *New York School Centers and Their Community Policy,* New York: Russell Sage Foundation, 1931.

Persons, W. Frank. *Welfare Council of New York City,* New York: Welfare Council, 1925.

Pettit, Walter W. *Case Studies in Community Organization,* New York: Century, 1928.

Pettit, Walter W. "The Relation of Social Work to Community Organization," *Journal of Social Forces,* VII, June, 1929.

Picht, Werner. *Toynbee Hall and the English Settlement Movement,* London: G. Bell and Sons, 1914.

Procter, Arthur W. *Financing of Social Work,* Chicago: A. W. Shaw, 1926.

Queen, Stuart A. *Social Work in the Light of History,* Philadelphia: Lippincott, 1922.

Queen, Stuart A. "What Is a Community?" *Social Forces,* I, May, 1923.

Reid, J. T. "Adult Education and Community Welfare," *Adult Education Journal,* II, October, 1943.

Remer, Alice W. "The East Boston School Center," *Social Forces,* V, September, 1926.

Renard, Blanche. "Uniform Districting in a Large City for Social and Civic Purposes," *Proceedings of the National Conference of Social Work, 1926,* Chicago: University of Chicago Press, 1926.

Report of the Cleveland Conference on District and Neighborhood Organization, December 7-8, 1947, New York: Community Chests and Councils, Inc., 1947.

"Report of the Committee on History of Charity Organization," *Proceedings of the National Conference of Charities and Correction, 1893,* Madison: Midland Publishing Co., 1893.

"Report and Plans for the Winter's Work," *University Settlement Society Bulletin,* November, 1893.

Richards, Wallace. "Community Groups and Neighborhood Planning," *Federator,* XIV, July, 1939.

Richmond, Mary E. "Some Methods of Charitable Co-operation I," *Charities,* VII, September, 1901.

Richmond, Mary E. "The Inter-Relation of Social Movements,"

Proceedings of the National Conference of Charities and Correction, 1910, Chicago: University of Chicago Press, 1910.

Riis, Jacob. *How the Other Half Lives,* New York: C. Scribner's Sons, 1890.

The Road to Community Reorganization, New York: The Woman's Foundation, 1945.

Robb, Lester A. "Neighborhood Coordinating Councils in Cincinnati," *Community Coordination,* IX, July-August, 1940.

Robinson, Duane. *Chance to Belong,* New York: Woman's Press, 1949.

Romano, Fred A. "Organizing a Community for Delinquency Prevention," *Yearbook of the National Probation Association, 1940,* New York: National Probation Association, 1940.

Rowden, D. and Kotinsky, R. "Community Organization and National Unity," *Journal of Adult Education,* XIII, June, 1941.

Sanderson, Dwight. "Community Organization for War and for Peace," *Social Forces,* October, 1942.

Scudder, Kenyon J. "The Co-ordinating Council at Work," *Yearbook of the National Probation Association, 1936,* New York: National Probation Association, 1936.

"The Settlement and Organized Charity," *Proceedings of the National Conference of Charities and Correction, 1896,* Boston: George H. Ellis, 1896.

"Settlements and Social Centers," *Social Forces,* VII, September, 1928.

Settlements and Their Outlook, New York: National Federation of Settlements, 1945.

"Settlements: To-day and the Future," *Survey,* LXXVIII, October, 1942.

Shaw, Clifford R. and Jacobs, Jesse. *The Chicago Area Project: An Experimental Program for the Prevention of Delinquency in Chicago,* Chicago: Illinois Institute for Juvenile Research, 1939 (Mimeographed).

Shaw, Clifford R. *Memorandum on Juvenile Delinquency* (Exhibit 4, pp. 540-547, Hearings before the U. S. Senate Sub-Committee on Wartime Health and Education, Juvenile Delinquency 1), Washington: U. S. Government Printing Office, 1944.

Shaw, Clifford R. *Preventing Juvenile Delinquency through Neighborhood Organization,* New York: Community Chests and Councils, Inc., 1947 (Mimeographed).

Sieder, Violet M. "Neighborhood Councils," *Community,* XXI, September, 1945.

Sieder, Violet M. "Public Welfare—Local Community Council Relationships," *New York State Conference on Social Work, 1945,* Syracuse: New York State Conference on Social Work, 1945.

Sieder, Violet M. "Grass Roots Under City Streets," *The Councillor,* Baltimore: Council of Social Agencies, June, 1946.

Sieder, Violet M. "Budgeting Is Planning in Action," *Community,* XXII, September, 1946.

Sieder, Violet M. "Neighborhood Councils," *Community,* XXII, October, 1946.

Sieder, Violet M. "Neighborhood Council Secretaries," *Community,* XXII, March, 1947.

Sieder, Violet M. "The Council Hopper," *Community,* XXII, June, 1947.

Sieder, Violet M. *Study of Area Projects of the Baltimore Youth Commission,* New York: Community Chests and Councils of America, Inc., March, 1949 (Mimeographed).

Simkhovitch, Mary K. "Neighborhood Planning and the Settlements," *The Survey,* LXXIX, June, 1943.

Smith, B. L. "Co-ordinated Community Group Action in Functional Adult Education," *Adult Education Bulletin,* VII, April, 1943.

Snedden, David, "Neighborhoods and Neighborliness," *Journal of Social Forces,* V, December, 1926.

"Social Settlements and the Labor Question," *Proceedings of the National Conference of Charities and Correction, 1896,* Boston: George H. Ellis, 1896.

"Social Union of the North and West Ends," *Charities and Commons,* XV, December, 1905.

Soule, Frederick J. "Settlements and Neighborhood Houses," *Social Work Year Book, 1947,* New York: Russell Sage Foundation, 1947.

South End House, Annual Report, Boston: 1909.

South End Association, Eighth Annual Report, Boston: January, 1900.

Springer, Gertrude. "Block-Aid," *The Survey,* LXVIII, May, 1932.

Stalley, Marshall. "The Church and the Community: the Story of the Overbrook, Pa., Community Council," *Federator*, XVI, September, 1941.

Stalley, Marshall. "Community Cooperation in Homewood Brushton," *Federator*, XIV, December, 1939.

Stalley, Marshall. "Council Executives Face New Responsibilities," *Community Coordination*, XI, May-June, 1941.

Stalley, Marshall. "Settlement Workers Discuss Neighborhood Councils," *Community Coordination*, VII, November-December, 1939.

Stark, Heman G. "Social Workers Discuss Coordinating Councils," *Community Coordination*, VIII, May-June, 1940.

Steiner, Jesse F. *The American Community in Action*, New York: Henry Holt and Co., 1928.

Steiner, Jesse F. "An Appraisal of the Community Movement," *Journal of Social Forces*, VII, March, 1929.

Steiner, Jesse F. *Community Organization*, New York: Century, 1925.

Steiner, Jesse F. "Community Organization: Myth or Reality," *American Sociological Society Publications*, XXIV, 1930.

Steiner, Jesse F. "Community Organization: A Study of its Rise and Tendencies," *Journal of Social Forces*, I, November, 1922.

Steiner, Jesse F. "Theories of Community Organization," *Journal of Social Forces*, III, November, 1924.

Steiner, Jesse F. "Whither the Community Movement?" *Survey*, LXII, April, 1929.

Stone, Walter L. *An Experiment in Neighborhood Planning and Community Research*, New York: Community Chests and Councils, Inc., Bulletin No. 81, April, 1935.

Stone, Walter L. "History of Development of Community Coordinating Councils," *Community Coordination*, IX, July-August, 1941.

Street, Elwood. "Community Organization in Greater St. Louis," *Journal of Social Forces*, VI, December, 1927.

Swift, Linton B. "Family Welfare Societies," *Social Work Year Book, 1929*, New York: Russell Sage Foundation, 1929.

Taft, Charles P. "National Defense and Community Service," *National Municipal Review*, XXX, June, 1941.

Taylor, Graham. "Social Tendencies of the Industrial Revolution," *The Commons*, IX, October, 1904.

Taylor, Graham. "Whither the Settlement Movement Tends," *Charities and The Commons,* XV, March, 1906.

Taylor, Lea D. "Social Settlements," *Social Work Year Book, 1935,* New York: Russell Sage Foundation, 1935.

Thrasher, Frederic M. *The Gang* (2nd Rev. ed.), Chicago: University of Chicago Press, 1936.

Thrasher, Frederic M. "Some Principles Underlying Community Co-ordination," *Journal of Educational Sociology,* XVIII, March, 1945.

Thrasher, Frederic M. "Juvenile Delinquency and Crime Prevention," *Journal of Educational Sociology,* VI, April, 1933.

Thrasher, Frederic M. "The Problem of Crime Prevention," *Yearbook of the National Probation Association, 1934,* New York: National Probation Association, 1934.

Thrasher, Frederic M. "Reaching Crime Causes by Coordinated Action," *Yearbook of the National Probation Association, 1936,* New York: National Probation Association, 1936.

Tibbits, Clark. "A Study of Chicago Settlements and Their Districts," *Social Forces,* VI, March, 1928.

Ward, Edward J. *The Social Center,* New York: Appleton, 1913.

Ward, Edward J. "The Southwestern School Center Conference," *Survey,* XXV, March, 1911.

Warner, Amos G., Queen, Stuart A., and Harper, Ernest B. *American Charities and Social Work,* New York: Crowell, 1930.

Watson, Frank D. *The Charity Organization Movement in the United States,* New York: Macmillan, 1922.

Waxter, Thomas J. S. "Baltimore's Area Projects," *Public Welfare,* LV, October, 1946.

Waxter, Thomas J. S. "Defense Councils and Permanent Welfare Agencies," *Proceedings of the National Conference of Social Work, 1943,* New York: Columbia University Press, 1943.

What Councils of Social Agencies Do, New York: Community Chests and Councils, Inc., Bulletin No. 100, 1939.

"What Remains for the Settlements?" *Survey,* XXXVI, June, 1916.

The Wheels of Organized Charity, Buffalo: Charity Organization Society, November, 1909.

White, Gaylord S. "Social Settlements After Twenty-five Years," *Harvard Theological Review,* IV, January, 1911.

White, Eva W. "Local Responsibility for Community Development," *Proceedings of the National Conference of Social Work, 1929,* Chicago: University of Chicago Press, 1929.

Winslow, Erving. "Philanthropic Individualism," *Survey,* XXXIV, September, 1915.

Witmer, Helen L. *Social Work,* New York: Farrar and Rinehart, 1942.

Wittenberg, Rudolph M. *Application of Group Work Principles to Voluntary Groups in the Community.* Paper presented at the National Conference of Social Work, 1947 (Mimeographed).

Wittenberg, Rudolph M. "Grass Roots and City Blocks," *Common Ground,* VII, Summer, 1947.

Woods, Robert A. (ed.). *The City Wilderness: A Settlement Study,* Boston: Houghton Mifflin Co., 1898.

Woods, Robert A. and Kennedy, Albert J. (eds.). *Handbook of Settlements,* New York: Charities Publication Committee, 1911.

Woods, Robert A. *The Neighborhood in Nation-Building,* Boston and New York: Houghton Mifflin Co., 1923.

Woods, Robert A. and Kennedy, Albert J. *The Settlement Horizon,* New York: Russell Sage Foundation, 1922.

Yourman, Julius. "Conference on Community Coordination," *Community Coordination,* VII, January-February, 1939.

Zander, Alvin F. "The Community Council," *Journal of Educational Sociology,* XIII, May, 1940.

Zehmer, G. B. "Adult Education for Community Betterment," *Adult Education Bulletin,* XI, October, 1946.

Zorbaugh, Harvey W. *The Gold Coast and the Slum,* Chicago: University of Chicago Press, 1929.

Zorbaugh, Harvey W. "The Natural Areas of the City," *American Journal of Sociology,* XXXII, July, 1926.

INDEX

185

New York City, Welfare Council of (*Cont.*)
  regional organization, 92, 138-139, 152
New York Community Council, Greater, 73
New York (state)
  Crime Commission, cited 106, 107
  Department of Education, Bureau of Adult Education, 134
New York State Citizens' Council, 134
Newstetter, Wilber I., cited 19n, 164
North, Cecil C., cited 102

Oakland (Calif.)
  Council of Social Agencies, 133
  School Department, 133

Paine, Robert Treat, Jr., cited 31
Pauperism, 29-32
Perry, Clarence A., cited 60n, 63, 76, 78, 85, 102
Persons, W. Frank, cited 92
Pettit, Walter, 70
Philadelphia (Pa.)
  charity organization in, 33-34
Phillips, Mr. and Mrs. Wilbur C., 80
Picht, Werner, cited 27
Pinchot, Gifford, 80
Pittsburgh (Pa.), 118, 121, 122
  social conditions, 45-46
  school centers, 63
  community councils, 99-100, 118-120, 154-155
  Joint Committee on Community Councils, 120
Pittsburgh and Allegheny County, Federation of Social Agencies of, 116, 118-120, 154-155
  Advisory Committee on Community Councils, 120
  Association of Community Councils, 120; cited 116
  Bureau of Community Councils, 154-155
Pittsburgh Associated Charities, 89
Pittsburgh, Social Study of, 119
Pittsburgh Survey, 45-46
Playground Association of America, 59

Poverty
  reduction of, 30

Queen, Stuart A., cited 25, 33, 68, 84

Recreation, 16, 124
Red Cross, American, 46, 71, 87, 124
Regionalism, 69
Richmond, Mary E., cited 32, 44, 48
Rochester (N.Y.)
  School Extension Committee, 59
  school centers, 59-60
Ruskin, John, 27
Russell Sage Foundation
  organization of, 45
  Department of Surveys and Exhibits, 46

St. John's College, Cambridge (England), 27
School
  cooperating with settlement, 102
  neighborhood organization role, 159-160
  objective, 47
  See also Education
School centers, 16
  beginnings, 47
  neighborhood organization, impetus of, 48
  objective, 47
  social integration by, 47
  starting points for defense councils, 48
  combating social disorganization, 58-59
  functions, 60
  definition, 76
  types, 60
  Wisconsin, 60
  number, 63
  community councils and, 63
  district improvement societies and, 63
  as centers of community organization, 71
  financial support of, 77
  community organization movement and, 78-79
  ideals, 78-79
  difficulties, 102
  after World War II, 132-133